A Common Hunger to Sing

A TRIBUTE TO SOUTH AFRICA'S BLACK WOMEN OF SONG 1950 TO 1990

Text by ZB Molefe
Photographs by Mike Mzileni
Introduction by Lara Allen

Kwela
BOOKS

The publishers wish to acknowledge the
indispensible contribution of Nedbank. Without its generous support this
publication would not have been possible in its present form.

The authors Z B Molefe and Mike Mzileni wish to
express their gratitude towards the
Foundation for the Creative Arts for funding their
travel expenses while researching and preparing the manuscript.

The Arts and Culture Trust of the President (ACT) envisages a society where everyone who has an interest in the arts, culture and heritage is provided with opportunities and resources to pursue it. This is inspired by an understanding that the cultural, artistic and spiritual needs of individuals and communities are as important as their needs for shelter, nutrition, clothing, health, education, work, safety and peace. By supporting the arts, culture and heritage, ACT makes a commitment to enhancing the quality of life of all South Africans.

ACT was founded by Nedbank, Sun International and the Ministry of Arts, Culture, Science and Technology. It is administered by a Board of Trustees consisting of personalities from the arts, culture, heritage and business communities. Its chief patron is President Nelson Mandela. Funds are derived from trust capital and products made available to people with an affinity for the arts, culture and heritage and a desire to support these. It is based on a partnership between business, the arts, culture and heritage in which all participants stand to prosper.

ACT provides financial and other assistance to projects in all the arts, culture and heritage forms. Merit and demonstrable need are key requirements. We aim to foster a sustainable cultural environment from which artists, heritage and cultural practitioners, as well as the public, can benefit. For ACT to succeed, support from the arts community, business, the public and government is needed. In turn, by supporting relevant projects, ACT makes it possible for the creative and aesthetic capacities of all participants to flourish in self-expression, exploration and reflection. Thus our lives may be enriched by the true upliftment, dignity, harmony, joy and splendour of that unique beauty which the arts, culture and heritage give to us.

In supporting this project, as well as others, ACT contributes towards creating a society in which we can fully participate in the cultural life of the community, enjoy the arts and benefit from them. This is the purpose of the Arts and Culture Trust of the President.

Message from Andries Oliphant, Chairperson of the Arts and Culture Trust of the President

Over the years, Nedbank has been involved in a number of arts and culture initiatives. The bank's involvement in the production of *A Common Hunger to Sing – A Tribute to South Africa's Black Women of Song, 1950 – 1990* is particularly significant in that it is in line with the bank's belief, that of making all genres of music and art accessible to all the people of South Africa.

It was with this in mind that, in 1994, Nedbank initiated (and continues to fund) the Arts and Culture Trust of the President, an organisation that supports exemplary developmental arts and culture projects. ACT helps to enrich cultural life in all communities by breaking down barriers and promoting mutual understanding, acceptance and reconciliation among all South Africans.

Apart from committing seed money to ACT, Nedbank has also developed a unique marketing strategy aimed at financially supporting ACT through a range of arts and culture affinity products. This approach has added value to the client by linking the use of affinity products such as cheque accounts, junior and adult savings accounts, ATM cards, credit cards (with the added bonus of being linked to SAA's frequent flyer programme, Voyager) and a distinctive "arts and culture" cell phone, to the support of a cause of the client's choice.

Nedbank's involvement in music, in particular with South Africa's female singers, spans many years. The bank has been involved with these singers both individually and as groups and has provided the launching pad for a successful career in a number of cases.

In the early 1990s, Nedbank worked with Queeneth Ndaba to put together *A Toast to the Ladies of Song,* a product of Dorkay House in Johannesburg, and a tribute to South Africa's female singers who faced hardship during the apartheid era. A number of South African female singers, including Sophie Mgcina, Jennifer Ferguson, Tandie Klaasen and Patience Africa, performed at this function. President Mandela and international singing star, Randy Crawford, attended this wonderful occasion.

Some years ago, Nedbank, in association with Gauteng premier Tokyo Sexwale, felt the need to honour black female singers by hosting a function at Johannesburg's Carlton Hotel. Top singers such as Margaret Singana (Mcingana), Dorothy Masuka and Dolly Rathebe attended.

Nedbank has also assisted a number of singers to produce and launch CDs. Recently Nedbank discovered Gloria Bosman and made it possible for her to study opera and music at the Pretoria Technikon.

From time to time Nedbank also brings in international talent to encourage cross-pollination of knowledge and talent between overseas artists and emerging South African artists. The bank brought the London Philharmonic Orchestra (LPO) to perform and conduct outreach programmes around the country. During this tour, Gcina Mhlope and Sibongile Khumalo worked extensively with the LPO.

In partially sponsoring the production of this book, Nedbank, through ACT, is fulfilling ACT's credo, which reads "We have a vision in which the minds and hearts of all South Africans will be opened, and stimulated to new understanding, by the arts in all their forms. We are proud that we can help expand cultural horizons by nurturing in all our people an appreciation of the arts and our country's rich heritage."

Nedbank believes that music is a wonderful form of artistic expression and communication. Accordingly, we feel that our stakeholders – our clients, staff and shareholders – are contributing towards encouraging emerging artists to aspire to appropriate role models.

There is no doubt that South Africa has a rich artistic heritage, which spans many decades. Nedbank would like to contribute towards a tribute to black South African female singers during the dark ages of apartheid. The bank sees this book as a fitting legacy.

We hope it will assist all South Africans to keep alive the history of African music and to inform future generations of the abundance of talent found in South Africa over the years.

Message from Richard Laubscher, Chief Executive of Nedbank

Contents

Foreword: An Affectionate Salute

A Common Hunger to Sing is a tribute to South Africa's black women of song, from the fifties to 1990.

This is our valentine. This is our paean, our affectionate salute to these remarkable women.

These are the singers who, in their own special way, forged the reality of their individual lives and in so doing made a significant contribution to urban black culture.

At funerals and wakes, in churches, schools, shebeens and community halls, they sang of the hopes, fears, dreams, pain and joy of their communities. In their unique way these oral historians, these social commentators, in styles that ranged from mbaqanga, simanje-manje, jazz and gospel to classical and pop, were fighting bigger battles than just trying to make a career as singers.

Our starting point is the fifties. It was an era of blossoming urban African music talent in South Africa. Audiences were seduced by a wide range of African singers who drew inspiration from an urban tradition born of their people who had been working in mines, brickyards, coal fields, factories, municipal services and doing domestic work in white residential areas in the changing South Africa of the early 20th century. Musical inspiration and influences were also exerted from overseas, particularly the United States. Ella Fitzgerald, Billie Holiday, Sarah Vaughan, Mahalia Jackson, Duke Ellington and Louis Armstrong, among a long list of other American musicians, are often cited by these women singers from Africa.

Suddenly urban black South Africa was flooded by various forms of music. The fifties saw the beginning of many music genres that would be played in the urban townships for decades to come. There was jazz, mbaqanga, kwela, choral music ...

But by the mid-fifties, this paradise of dance, music and song was radically transformed. The National Party government, which came to power in 1948, had irretrievably altered the very fibre of South African society with rigid apartheid policies. The relatively calm urban African tempo of the forties changed at the stroke of the apartheid government pen.

This was when these singers – who like millions of other Africans all over South Africa suddenly found their movements restricted and activities regulated by government permits and controlled by an intrusive and pervasive police presence – brought hope where there was despair.

There would be better tomorrows for their people, their songs intoned.

They built on the musical legacy left by the long line of illustrious singers who preceded them, including Emily Kwenane, Emily Motsieloa, Faith Caluza, Lindi Makhanya and Marie Dube.

Also on the heritage of Snowy Radebe (Mahlangu) and Marjorie Pretorius, who strictly speaking belong to the forties, but whom we are fortunate to be able to include in this book.

Some of the women featured here went on to conquer the world: Miriam Makeba, Letta Mbulu, Sophie Mgcina, Sathima Bea Benjamin, Dorothy Masuka, Thuli Dumakude, Busi (Viccie) Mhlongo and the Mahotella Queens ...

There were, however, also those singers who kept the home fires burning. Particularly in the eighties, when, within South Africa and without, it was not yet clear that the demise of apartheid was imminent and inevitable. International opinion against apartheid South Africa had hardened by then. The international cultural boycott had intensified. Culturally and artistically, South Africa was effectively cut off from the rest of the world.

But Dolly Rathebe, Joy, Sibongile Khumalo, Yvonne Chaka Chaka, Tandie Klaasen, Rebecca Malope, Brenda Fassie, among a legion of black women singers, stand out as beacons of light in those dark days.

Like "A Salute and Toast to the Ladies of the Fifties", the concert presented in the Johannesburg Civic Theatre on March 8, 1993, and the series of concerts, "Africa's Women of Song", at Johannesburg's then premier jazz club, Kippies, at the end of July 1996, we wish to pay tribute to these great artists.

We hope that this book will be viewed as a permanent record of the achievements of the leading

African women singers of four crucial decades in South Africa. As to its inevitable gaps, here and there, we plead that our humble, modest contribution be regarded as an introduction for those who want to discover what role black urban women played in the struggle for a democratic South Africa, particularly in the performing arts.

The vast majority of singers fit into the popular and jazz sphere, but one opera singer we simply could not leave out: Isabella Masote.

We would have loved to include the amazing young opera star Sibongile Mngoma as well, but she came into her own only after 1990.

In the tradition of Kate Manye, her sister Charlotte and the African Jubilee Singers, who were presented at the court of England's Queen Victoria in 1891, and more recently Patty Nokwe and Sibongile Khumalo, these women dared to be different and entered a field some people mistakenly believed was the preserve of whites.

Interviewing and photographing the singing stars featured in this book was a humbling experience. Most of the interviews were done in 1993, when Nelson Mandela had been released but the first democratic elections in the country had not yet been peacefully conducted. We were living on the edge, times were stressful, and it was touching to listen to their stories as they opened their hearts, giving of their inner hopes, dreams, triumphs and disappointments in their different music careers.

Their stories, their voices, the rhythms of their telling were as varied and compelling as the personalities themselves. But a thread, a pattern, runs throughout their stories: a common hunger to sing. Theirs is music that informs, rectifies, laments and rejoices in the rich tapestry that was and is their world.

Our intention is that these stories must be accessible to as many people as possible. Hence our approach was, from the outset, to allow our subjects to tell their stories themselves. There was very little editing, except for clarity, story flow, length and context. Naturally the stories were updated where necessary.

In a few cases we were compelled to use published and broadcast sources. This was the result of a combination of factors beyond our control, ranging from some of the singers' refusal to be interviewed, to another demanding that she be paid and the manager of a third refusing to let his charge be interviewed.

The photographs, except for shots of performances, were specially taken for this book. They tell their own story.

We beg forgiveness for those singers whose contribution we could acknowledge but who could not be featured on their own. People like Francisca Mngomezulu, Esther Khoza and Emma Seneke, who are deceased; Louisa Emmanuel and Pinise Saul, who live abroad and who could not be photographed; Dixie Kwankwa, Helen van Rensburg and Nancy Jacobs who have lost interest in their musical past.

The preparation of this book has been an education and we want to share this treasure trove of South African urban culture with the greatest range of South Africans, as well as music lovers elsewhere.

The biggest bouquets belong to Queeneth Ndaba, administrator of the Dorkay House Trust, Johannesburg; singers Abigail Kubeka, Letta Mbulu and Sathima Bea Benjamin. When this project was at its infancy they blessed it, encouraged us and insisted that it had to be finished "by all means necessary".

Our sincere thanks to Lara Allen for her wonderfully elucidating essay. It is only fitting that a woman should have given us the big picture and put the musical contribution of her sisters in perspective.

Z B MOLEFE
Johannesburg, July 1997

Introduction:
South African Women of Song, their Lives and Times[1]

Miriam Makeba, Dolly Rathebe, Dorothy Masuka. These are the names which immediately come to mind at the mention of our heritage of great women singers. They were the bright lights of the fifties, the first Hollywood-style stars. The history of black South African stage women, however, goes back much further than the fifties. It goes right back least to the beginning of Euro-American-inspired urban popular music: those first occasions when people sang and made music purely to entertain, rather than as part of working or religious life, or "traditional" communal celebrations. Although men have tended to dominate the making of popular music, in numbers as well as in terms of creative and organisational control, each era has borne a small active group of feisty, creative women who, often against immense odds, have raised their voices in song.

This tribute volume presents photographic and textual portraits of over fifty South African singers. Since the textual portraits are personal testimonies in which singers constantly, and without explanation, refer to each other and to shared experiences and events, the uninitiated reader might easily become baffled. With this introduction, therefore, I attempt to provide a base, a map to aid the exploration of the rest of the book. It is a brief historical overview of the activities of black South African women singers over the past century. It is a who-did-what-and-when, with a little bit of why-and-how. Since more than half of the singers featured enjoyed their heyday during the fifties and sixties, I have concentrated on this period. I have also concentrated on the Gauteng region for, largely because the recording industry is based there, Johannesburg is the city of gold for musicians also. Although the rest of South Africa has produced many excellent musicians, many have moved to Johannesburg in order to further their careers.

Unfortunately much of the music produced by these singers is no longer available. Re-issues of some material have, however, recently been released on compact disc and I have made a note of these recordings for the benefit of readers who would also like to become listeners. Staying true to the spirit of

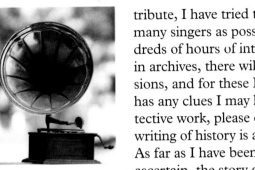

tribute, I have tried to acknowledge as many singers as possible but, despite hundreds of hours of interviews and months in archives, there will inevitably be omissions, and for these I apologise. If anyone has any clues I may have missed in my detective work, please come forward. The writing of history is an ongoing process! As far as I have been able to ascertain, the story goes like this ...

The first stage performances by black artists to attract media attention in South Africa were minstrel shows, largely inspired by Orpheus McAdoo's African-American troupe, the Virginia Jubilee Singers, who toured South Africa in the 1890s. In 1891 a South African minstrel troupe, the African Jubilee Singers (also called the South African Choir), went to England. About half the group were women, including two sisters, Charlotte and Kate Manye.[2]

The next high-profile visits to Britain by South African musicians occurred in 1930, this time stimulated by the fledgling South African recording industry. Two record companies were competing to produce black popular music for the local market and, since there were no recording studios in South Africa until 1932, musicians were sent to England to cut their discs. His Master's Voice signed a contract with premier choir leader and composer Reuben Caluza, who recorded 150 songs with his Double Quartette.[3] In the same year Eric Gallo's Singer Gramophone Company sent Griffiths Motsieloa to London, where he recorded a number of songs with Ignatius Monare. In 1931 Motsieloa returned with a larger group and made a number of recordings as Griffiths Motsieloa and Company.[4]

On his return to South Africa Motsieloa established the Merry Blackbirds who, under the leadership of Peter Rezant, were to become the most prestigious elite dance band of the thirties and forties. The Merry Blackbirds, with Emily Motsieloa on piano, was the first band to boast a female vocalist, the young Marjorie Pretorius. Later the Jazz Maniacs, the Merry Blackbirds' main competitors, employed vocalist Emily Kwenane. The Merry Blackbirds distinguished themselves by playing exclusively

American big-band swing which they read from sheet music, while other contemporary bands played mostly by ear and included South African compositions in their repertoire. Thoughout the century black South African musicians have held African-American musicians in great esteem and American, particularly African-American, musical styles have strongly influenced the development of South African popular music. The American influence is evident in both the music and the lyrics. Most singers have been inspired and influenced by their famous African-American counterparts and many have recorded both in their home tongue and in English.

The thirties and forties was the great age of vaude-ville in South Africa, and again Griffiths Motsieloa presided over the premiere company, the Pitch Black Follies. Women were vital in the song-and-dance variety format of vaudeville and, except for those vocalists who sang with dance bands, most female performing artists of this era built their careers on the vaudeville stage. The leading lights of the Pitch Black Follies were Lindi Makhanya, Eleanor and Babsy Oliphant and Snowy Radebe.[5] Although unusual, it was not unheard of for women to lead and manage their own vaudeville troupes. One of Durban's most prominent companies from the mid-forties to the early fifties was the Streamline Sisters ("brothers" were also included), which was founded and directed by Paulina Philips. Other troupes led by women included the Madcaps from Mafeking founded by Mrs S M Molema; the Movietone Cabaret Girls led by Florence K Nthatisi of Bloemfontein; the Raven Girls of Pretoria managed by Mrs L Kgokong; Miss V N Plaatje's Rhythm Girls of Kimberley; and the all-female Merry Makers of Bloemfontein who were led and managed by Johanna Phahlane, also an outspoken journalist and women's rights activist.[6]

One vaudeville troupe which profoundly affected the development of South African music and theatre was the Synco Fans, led by teacher, composer and pianist Wilfred Sentso. Established in the mid-thirties, the Synco Fans performed throughout South Africa for more than twenty years, but the troupe's primary importance lies in the fundamental role it played as a training institution. Top vocalists of the thirties and forties Margorie Pretorius and Emily Kwenane started off in the Synco Fans, as did fifties recording stars Martha Mdenge and Mabel Mafuya.[7] The Synco Fans' principal female star during the forties and early fifties was Suzanne Seeku.[8]

The other troupe to function well into the mid-fifties, and which literally linked thirties and forties vaudeville with the grand variety shows of the fifties,[9] was the Gay Gaieties. Led by James Tutie, the Gay Gaieties also provided an initial training platform for young artists. The most famous singer to have started her career with this troupe is Tandie Klaasen, known then as Tandie Mpambani. Tandie is probably the single greatest survivor of the South African stage. A well-known singer, dancer, comedienne and stage personality of the forties and fifties, she went to London with *King Kong*. On her return she continued her singing career throughout the dark years of high apartheid, when many others gave up. Tandie sang through political difficulties and great personal tragedy and is today still one of South Africa's most sought-after jazz and cabaret artists.[10]

There is a strong tendency these days to romanticise the fifties as a golden era, brimful of jazz and glamour, hope and confidence, humour and style. It was that time before the full onslaught of apartheid, when the ANC became a mass-based movement and the people took to the streets protesting peacefully, Ghandi-style against unjust laws. It was also the era of flamboyant and witty journalists, suave American-style gangsters and sophisticated singing stars.

Nurtured by the newly initiated pictorial press (publications like *Zonk!*, *Golden City Post*, and particularly *Drum*), the fifties boasted an almost explosive flowering of black popular culture. *Drum* and its sister publications provided a cultural focus for city dwellers, an outlet for a new generation of writers and photographers, and a medium through which top personalities in music, theatre and sport became Hollywood-type stars.[11] Anxious to grace their pages with pictures of beautiful women (so much the better if they were also interesting and cre-ative), pictorials like *Drum* gave women singers a great deal of space, substantially bolstering their careers. Top singers like Dolly Rathebe, Dorothy Masuka and Miriam Makeba became household names, no longer just musicians but also cover girls and leaders of fashion, icons of glamour and sophis-tication.

Dolly Rathebe, the first of this generation of stars, initially rose to fame on the wings of the fledgling local film industry. When the cream of Johannesburg's talent gathered for the 1949 auditions for the first South African all-black film, *Jim Comes to Jo'burg*, no one guessed that an unknown, scruffy young girl from Sophiatown would win the lead role and shortly become the doyenne of black showbiz. The other female film stars of the fifties were Mabel Magada and Ribbon Dlamini, who took lead roles in *Song of Africa* and *Cry, the Beloved Country* respectively. However, neither enjoyed Dolly Rathebe's exceptional vocal skills, and their careers faded when the film industry slumped. Dolly starred in a 1951 feature film, *The Magic Garden*, and then went on to sing with the Reef's top bands, touring as far as Cape Town and Lourenço Marques (now Maputo) with such groups as the Manhattan Stars, the African Inkspots and the Harlem Swingsters. She appeared in Alf Herbert's *African Jazz and Variety* show when it opened in 1954 and remained his top attraction for years. Dolly retired from the stage in the mid sixties, only to make a resounding comeback two decades later. Her recent film career includes such credits as *Mapantsula* and the most recent version of *Cry, the Beloved Country*. As a soloist with the Elite Swingsters, she performs regularly both nationally and internationally and has recorded several albums.[12]

Besides the stage and screen, the other popular-culture medium which boomed in the fifties was sound recording. Although 78 r.p.m. shellac records were available in South Africa from the early 1900s, and local black musicians were recorded from the thirties, only in the fifties did the Johannesburg-based local music industry start to explore and exploit the enormous music-hungry black urban market. The first studio to produce a top female recording star was Troubadour Records when in 1953 they recorded a young Zimbabwean girl singing her own composition, "Hamba Notsokolo". This song launched Dorothy Masuka's career: it became an instant hit and has since become a South African classic. Her talent for composition sets Dorothy apart from most other singers, and her style, a unique blend of African and American musical elements that she calls Masuka music, inspired and influenced other singers and song-writers throughout the fifties and sixties.[13] In 1961 Dorothy flew to Zimbabwe after making a politically sensitive recording. She was not permitted to return to South Africa for thirty years.

Troubadour's other star vocalist was Mabel Mafuya who, with her group the Green Lanterns, produced many hit records during the fifties. At times during this period Troubadour is reputed to have controlled up to 75% of the African record market, an extraordinary percentage largely due to the exceptional commercial, artistic and organisational skills and instincts of talent scout Cuthbert Matumba. Matumba was renowned for having recordings in the market place within twenty-four hours, and for maintaining an "open door policy" (meaning that he was prepared to record "underground" sessions with musicians contracted to other companies). Another of Matumba's unusual methods was that he employed his own musicians and vocalists on a permanent basis, paying them per week rather than per recording, as was the norm in other studios.[14] A regular, decent wage and job security was almost unheard of for musicians in those days. Until well into the seventies most black musicians received a flat fee for each song they recorded and, in the process, unwittingly lost their royalty rights.

Motivated by Troubadour's successes with Dorothy and Mabel, competing record companies sought their own female stars. EMI talent scout Rupert Bopape "discovered" Susan Gabashane, while the bright lights in Strike Vilakazi's stable at Trutone Records were Martha Mdenge and Nancy Jacobs. The latter recorded the original version of "Meadowlands", which later became the popular anthem of the Sophiatown removals.[15] Strike Vilakazi also recorded the first "girl group" to become recording stars, the Quad Sisters. In 1952 Tandie Mpambani (Klaasen) decided to challenge the popularity of male close-harmony groups like the Manhattan Brothers and the African Ink Spots and, with her sister Thandeka, formed the all-female Quad Sisters. "I was just tired of men thinking they can do better than us. I said anything you can do, we can do it better."[16]

The decade's finest female close-harmony exponents were, however, the Skylarks, a group formed by Miriam Makeba in 1956 in response to a request from Gallo talent scout Sam Alcock. Initially the group included Miriam's sister Mizpah Makeba, Johanna Radebe and Helen van Rensburg. It was, however, the core line-up of Miriam Makeba, Mary Rabotapi, Mummy Girl Nketle and Abigail Kubeka, occasionally joined by Nomunde Sihawu and bass Sam Ngakane, who recorded the Skylarks' greatest hits during the late fifties.[17] In 1959 Miriam left South Africa to pursue her career abroad. Since she left in order to appear at the Venice Film Festival, to which she had been invited as a result of her appearance in Lionel Rogosin's anti-apartheid film *Come Back Africa*, it was necessary that she be quietly spirited out of the country. She said farewell her own way:

through her last recording with the Skylarks titled "Miriam's Goodbye to Africa".[18]

When Abigail and Mary returned from the London run of *King Kong* they tried to revive the Skylarks. They invited various promising singers to lead, including the young Letta Mbulu, but it soon became clear that the Skylarks could not be the Skylarks without Miriam, and the group separated. The only member who managed to retain a performance career throughout the seventies and eighties was Abigail Kubeka. Versatility, Abigail explains, is the secret of her survival and her success. "I was a singer, an actress, a model. I had to do all those things. Thank goodness I could!"[19] With experience in television, film, musical theatre, jazz and cabaret, Abigail is still one of the country's top entertainers.

While film and recording presented new scope for performers in the fifties, the traditional venue for singers, the stage, continued to offer opportunities and employment. During and after the Second World War a white officer, Lieutenant Ike Brooks, heralded a new era when he assembled a company of black servicemen and, playing to racially mixed audiences, toured South Africa with a musical revue titled *Zonk!*[20] The new epoch in black showbusiness, however, really started in 1954 when white impresario Alfred Herbert produced his first *African Jazz and Variety* show at the Windmill Theatre in downtown Johannesburg. Black vaudeville troupes had been delighting black audiences with variety entertainment for over two decades; Herbert's contribution was to initiate the first large-scale, high-profile, on-going performances of black artists mostly for white audiences. The *African Jazz and Variety* roster read like a Who's Who of black showbiz. The female vocalists who received top billing in the show's heyday were Dolly Rathebe, Dorothy Masuka, Tandie Mpambani (Klaasen), Louisa Emmanuel and Rose Mathyse, closely followed by Barbara Brown, Freda Ryce and Joyce Seneke. Their male counterparts included Ben "Satch" Masinga, Isaac Peterson, Gene Williams, Sonny Pillay, the Cuban Brothers and the Woody Woodpeckers. In 1956 Herbert introduced a new variety element through the inclusion of "snake dancer" Rose Hlela, a role fulfilled in subsequent years by ex-beauty queens Dotty Tiyo and Irene Batchelor. Provocative dance gradually became more important and in the early sixties Herbert aptly renamed his show *African Follies*, for it now contained more legs and dancing than jazz and variety.

Herbert was a compulsive gambler which, particularly when he lost his company's weekly wages, opened him to accusations of exploitation. But according to such stalwarts of his show as Dolly, Dorothy and Tandie, a particular loyalty and trust existed between Herbert and his artists. They understood when he was unable to pay their wages on time, knowing that they would not have to wait long, while he in turn lent or gave cast members money when they were in need. Whatever his failings, for over a decade Herbert provided regular employment and facilitated recognition beyond the townships for a large number of artists. For this he is fondly remembered by many members of his show. "We loved him," says Dolly Rathebe. "Mr Herbert made people what they are."[21]

In 1956 the Union of Southern African Artists presented a series of variety concerts in competition with Herbert's *African Jazz*. Commonly called Union Artists, this organisation was formed in the mid-fifties to protect the interests of black musicians, actors and actresses. The first of the Union Artists variety concerts was a grand event organised to say thank you and farewell to Father Huddleston, the much-loved and respected Anglican priest who, through his untiring social and political activism, had improved the lives of so many Sophiatown inhabitants. The money raised on this occasion was used to purchase premises for the Union at Dorkay House in downtown Johannesburg, which served as a nucleus for music and theatre throughout the sixties and seventies.[22] The ensuing shows organised by Ian Bernhardt were titled *Township Jazz* and starred the Manhattan Brothers, Miriam Makeba, the Skylarks and Thoko Thomo who, with the male close-harmony group Lo Six, had just burst onto the scene with a hit recording, "Thoko Shukuma". Two years previously the Manhattan Brothers, the country's premiere close-harmony group with twenty years' experience, effectively launched Miriam Makeba's career when they took her on as their female vocalist.

By the late fifties the variety-show format had become stale and Union Artists turned their attention to a more ambitious project: the production of the first black South African musical, *King Kong*.[23] Based on the true life (and death) story of heavyweight boxing champion Ezekiel Dhlamini, *King Kong* took South Africa by storm. After playing to sell-out audiences in Johannesburg for six weeks it embarked on a successful nation-wide tour. Miriam

Makeba played Joyce, King Kong's shebeen-queen girlfriend, whilst Manhattan Brothers Nathan Mdledle and Joe Mogotsi took the male lead roles: *King Kong* and Lucky the gangster respectively.[24]

The overwhelming success of *King Kong* in South Africa attracted British promoters and the show was booked for a London run. Adaptations were made to the script and music, and in 1960 auditions were held for the London version. One of the most important changes was the casting of Peggy Phango (whose previous experience included *African Jazz* and *Cry, the Beloved Country*) as leading lady Joyce. Miriam Makeba was unavailable because after her appearance at the Venice Film Festival she travelled to the United States where, as a protégé of Harry Belafonte, she was enjoying a successful solo career. The London version of *King Kong* was the first big break for Sophie Mgcina who, as a singer, actress, composer and teacher, was to become a leading figure in South African music for the next thirty years.[25]

Although often seen as a glorious end to a golden era, the final curtain of *King Kong* did not signal the end of South African musical theatre. *King Kong*'s success in fact stimulated the production of many local musicals throughout the sixties, notably Alan Paton's *Sponono*, starring Ruth Nkonyeni, and *Back In Your Own Backyard*, produced by Ben "Satch" Masinga under the auspices of Union Artists. The female lead in this production was Letta Mbulu, who shortly afterwards emigrated to the United States, where she enjoyed a long, successful career in exile.[26]

Union Artists also provided the initial inspiration and training for the most influential figure in South African musical theatre, Gibson Kente. In 1963 he wrote, produced, directed and starred in his first musical, *Manana the Jazz Prophet*. His female leads were Letta Mbulu, Jeanette Tsagane and Bridget "Snowy" Gwabini (Peterson). Gibson Kente consistently produced musicals inspired by township life for the next thirty years, the best known being *Sikalo*; *How Long*; *Zwi* and *Lifa*. Playing in converted beer halls, township halls and cinemas all over the country, Gibson Kente's productions became the drama school for black South African music and theatre. Almost everyone who became anyone during the next three decades spent apprenticeship time in his cast. "Some people found working for Gibson difficult because he never had a sponsor and couldn't pay much," says Zakithi Dlamini, who starred in

Kente's productions for twenty-five years. "But he was good. He'd write the play, direct it, design sets for it, costumes for it, do the choreography, all on his own. You learnt a lot being with him."[27]

In contrast to Kente's urban township versions of the American musical, the sixties saw the birth of a new genre of musical theatre: the grand African spectacle. Such shows tended to consist largely of "tribal" singing and dancing, often featuring many bare-breasted "Zulu" maidens. Such an aural and visual spectacle was generally presented through a narrative which presented rural values and traditions as pure and noble in contrast to the corrupted morals and troubled lives of city dwellers. The first high-profile show of this type was Bertha Egnos's production of *Dingaka* in 1961, which was made into a film by Jamie Uys in 1963. Although such shows tended to endorse certain apartheid values (such as those underscoring the homelands policies), they did generate employment for singers and dancers at a time when work was hard to come by, and the opportunities they presented launched the careers of several artists. Patience Africa's career, for instance, started when she was brought from Durban to appear in the film version of *Dingaka*, while Mara Louw's big break came when she toured locally and internationally with *Meropa* between 1973 and 1976. Although Thembi Mtshali had already toured internationally with *Meropa* and Welcome Msomi's *uMabatha*, her first major lead role was Mama Tembu in Bertha Egnos's early seventies production *Ipi Tombi*, probably the most famous show within its genre.

By the eighties the Market Theatre in Johannesburg had become a home for progressive and experimental performing arts. At this venue, for the first time in twenty years, black artists could perform for white or racially mixed audiences on a regular basis. Among the many ground-breaking productions created for the Market Theatre were *Poppie Nongena* and *Singing the Times*. Initially produced at the Market Theatre in 1980, *Poppie Nongena* was re-staged in New York in 1982, with the title role played by Thuli Dumakude. Much of the credit for the production's success, however, goes to Sophie Mgcina, who not only played two lead roles but was musical director and dialogue coach and also composed the music.[28] Written by Tu Nokwe, *Singing the Times* was a dramatised representation of her mother's life story. Through speech, dance and song, Patty Nokwe, with her two daughters Tu and Marylin, enacted the story of Patty's life and career as a young singer in Durban during the fifties. Thembi Mtshali, Thoko Ntshinga and Nomsa Nene appeared regularly in Market Theatre productions throughout the eighties, while one of the most promising young male actors, Mbongeni Ngema, went on to produce several musicals including *Sarafina*, which launched Leleti Khumalo's stage and film career.

While their sisters were building stage careers, many singers in the sixties, seventies and eighties went into recording. When the Skylarks disbanded in the early sixties their place as top women's close-harmony group was already being challenged. A new sound was developing in the EMI studios under the watchful eye of talent scout/producer Rupert Bopape, his vanguard group being the highly successful Dark City Sisters. They sang a brand of vocal jive which (although influenced both by the American-style vocal swing of the Skylarks and Dorothy's more African-sounding "Masuka music") stylistically fore-shadowed the coming of mbaqanga. To begin with, the Dark City Sisters were a name, a concept, and although Joyce Mogatusi sang the lead part on most recordings, the other Sisters seem to have been drawn fairly arbitrarily from Bopape's EMI stable. It was only when the group became famous and fans started clamouring for live concerts by their idols that membership of the Dark City Sisters was con-solidated. The core group which performed live during the early sixties consisted of Joyce Mogatusi (leader), Grace Msika, Esther Khoza and Hilda Mogapi. When Hilda left she was replaced by Audrey Zwane.[29] Different combinations of these singers also recorded for EMI as the Flying Jazz Queens, the Black Sea Giants, and the Killingstone Stars.[30]

In 1964 Bopape left EMI for Gallo, where he culti-vated a roster of musicians who developed the driving, upbeat sound of sixties mbaqanga. The pioneers of instrumental mbaqanga were Gallo's premier backing group, the Makhona Tsohle Band, who devised a style influenced by "traditional" music, but using electric instruments. They backed the leaders of vocal mbaqanga (sometimes called mqashiyo or simanje-manje), Mahlatini and the Mahotella Queens. The combination of Simon "Mahlathini" Nkabinde's roaring ultra-deep bass with the high close-harmony style of the Mahotella Queens proved exceptionally successful, and the ensemble dominated township music until the end of the decade. The only group which seriously challenged the Mahotella Queens was Izintombi Zesi Manje Manje, led by Jane Dhlamini. In 1986 Mahlatini and the Mahotella Queens with the Makhona Tsohle Band staged a come-back and en-joyed an active international career for the next decade.[31]

Membership of the Mahotella Queens is even more difficult to discern than it is with the Dark City Sisters. The issue is so complex and controversial that in the early nineties there were two separate groups of singers performing as the Mahotella Queens.[32] Like the Dark City Sisters, the Mahotella Queens was initially just one of the names under which singers in the Gallo stable recorded. Different combinations of the same singers recorded under such other names as the Dima Sisters, the Sweet Home Dames, the Mthunzini Girls and Izintombi Zomoya. The explanation given is that, since singers earned a flat fee per song recorded, this arrangement ensured that they were able to earn a living, for the market would accept only a certain number of releases by a particular group within a year. Once the Mahotella Queens started appearing live at shows, however, personnel changes became less frequent. During the sixties the Mahotella Queens consisted of four or five at any one time of the following core of singers: Ethel Mgomezulu, Hilda Tloubatla, Juliet Mazamisa, Nunu Maseko, Windy Sebeko, Mildred Mangxola and Nobesuthu Shawe.[33]

During the seventies male groups started to domi-nate vocal mbaqanga and the popular music market was engulfed by a wave of soul, both foreign and local. However, although South African soul remained largely a male domain, several women vocalists did make their mark performing with the top soul groups. Eaglet Ditse, for instance, sang for the Beaters, while Dinah Mbatha joined Blondie Makhene as the Movers' front vocalist. Both Margaret Singana (Mgcingana) and Mavis Maseko sang with Drive. It was, however, Margaret Singana who made the most impact as a soloist during the seventies. With such runaway hits as "I Never Loved a Man" and "Stand by Your Man", she earned the title "Lady Africa".[34] In 1979 a trio called Joy (Thoko Ndlozi, Anneline Malebu, and Felicia Marion) won stardom overnight with the pop-soul number "Paradise Road". When the group disbanded, Felicia went into gospel, Thoko became one of Miriam Makeba's backing singers and Anneline formed another trio with Tshidii Le Loka and Faith Kekana called Shadiii.

Late in 1983 Brenda Fassie and her band the Big Dudes took South Africa by storm with "Weekend Special".[35] With this single Brenda launched the township disco era and remained the unassailable queen of township pop throughout the eighties. The only other songstress to attain pop royalty status was Yvonne Chaka Chaka, who exploded onto the scene in 1985 with "I'm in Love with a DJ".[36] Loved and adored throughout the continent, Yvonne became known as "Princess of Africa". The important male figures in township pop were Sello "Chicco" Twala and Dan Tshanda. Both, in the roles of producer and composer, nurtured other successful township pop artists. Dan Tshanda attained his greatest successess with Splash, Patricia Majalisa and the Dalom Kids while, as Chimora, Chicco's backing trio became a top-selling group in its own right.

Township disco, often called "bubblegum", made such an enormous impact that for almost a decade the major record companies refused to record any other style for the pop market. All aspirant singers therefore had to record disco and although some, like Ebony (Lena Khama), Vicky Sampson and Mercy Pakela were successful, many artists complain that this stylistic monopoly stifled their creativity and careers. Even gospel queen Rebecca Malope was made to sing disco when she first started recording in 1987. Eventually Rebecca signed with a new record company and, with her 1992 release *Rebecca Sings Gospel*, revolutionised the recording of South African religious music.[37]

In the early nineties audiences, tired of the bubblegum sound, switched their allegiances to international fare and local sales fell drastically. In an attempt to reclaim their market, South African musicians and producers experimented with local versions of various imported forms. The most successful development was South African gospel, pioneered by Rebecca Malope, although Sister Phumi was also successful with her gospel-reggae sound. Several male artists and groups explored the possibilities of local rap and ragga, a trend which in 1994 developed into a style called kwaito. A South Africanised blend of international dance musics such as house, techno and hip hop, kwaito took the townships by storm. The most prominent women in the kwaito scene are Lebo Mathosa and Thembi Seete from Boom Shaka, and Abashante who dance and sing with "kwaito king" Arthur Mafokate.

Until very recently singers committed to expressing themselves in styles beyond the commercial mainstream (such as jazz, afro-fusion and crossover) were largely ignored by the South African recording industry. The only South African female vocalist who has managed to build a career singing "pure" American-style jazz is Sathima Bea Benjamin. Most of her albums were recorded and released in the United States where she lived for more than thirty years in exile. Furthermore, when Busi Mhlongo (a promising young singer on the local circuit during the sixties) returned from twenty years of exile in Europe, she was unable to find a South African company prepared to record her passionate and distinctive blend of "traditional" African and contemporary sounds. Her album *Babhemu* was eventually recorded in the Netherlands in 1994 and was listed among the top ten World Music albums in Europe.[38] The 1996 releases of two adventurous recordings suggest, however, that local recording companies may be changing their tactics. Both albums, *Ancient Evenings* by Sibongile Khumalo and *Inyakanyaka* by Tu Nokwe, have been "in preparation" since the late eighties and, in different ways, creatively explore the fusion of jazz, "traditional" and commercial musical elements.[39]

One of the best-kept secrets about music-making in South African is the extent to which black musicians and audiences are involved in the performance and appreciation of western classical music. Black choirs have boasted largely, often exclusively, classical repertoires since the end of the nineteenth century, and over the years many gifted singers have risen through the ranks to become soloists. Today our black divas like Sibongile Khumalo, Sibongile Mngoma and Isabella Masote are recognised and fêted. Career and performance opportunities are available. When, for instance, Linda Bukhosini and her husband Bongani Tembe recently returned from New York, where they studied classical singing, they were employed by the Playhouse Company (formerly the Natal Performing Arts Council) and are actively involved in the administration and performance of music in KwaZulu-Natal. Their predecessors were not so fortunate. Over the years KwaZulu-Natal has exported many fine classical singers: Between 1949 and 1955 alone, John Ngcobo, Victor Mcunu, Ignatius Temba and Doreen Mzobe set sail for England to further their careers. A few years later Patty Nokwe (then Masuku) was offered the chance to futher her classical training in Italy, but for various reasons decided not to follow up the opportunity.

Throughout the century musical performance has been an arena bounded by firmly entrenched gender roles. Women sing, men play instruments. There have, however, been some notable exceptions. The first famous woman instrumentalist was Emily Motsieloa, who was the Merry Blackbirds' pianist for two decades from the thirties. In the late thirties the Jazz Maniacs, Johannesburg's other top big band, briefly employed a woman pianist, Hope Khumalo.[40] Pianists did not generally excite a great deal of comment since, if a woman had to play an instrument, the piano was by far the most acceptable. However, when singer Lynette Leeuw made some recordings on the alto saxophone in 1963 she caused a media sensation. In the mid-eighties Queen of Ndebele music Nothembi Mkwebane broke a double taboo when she started recording.[41] Not only was she one of the first women stars within the realm of neo-traditional music, but she also played the guitar. Before Nothembi the guitar was played by men only.

Resistance to their playing instruments was not the only problem women musicians had to contend with. Other difficulties reverberate thematically throughout the following testimonies. Stage women have, for instance, long had to battle against social attitudes which categorise them as loose or wild. Many singers therefore experienced strong resistance from their parents and families, who wanted them to take up more respectable, reliable professions, such as teaching or nursing. The problem which caused the most heartache, however, was the conflict of interests which so often arose between trying to balance the "traditional" role of a "good wife" with a stage career. The lucky few who managed to be successful wives and singers generally had understanding, supportive husbands who helped raise the children and were not fearful or jealous of their wife's fame and exposure. Most singers, however, had to choose. Some gave up the stage, others lost their husbands. Then of course there were the problems shared by both male and female musicians. Everyone suffered economic exploitation at the hands of promoters and record companies. But most destructive of all was the way in which apartheid legislation (such as the Separate Amenities Act, the Group Areas Act, the liquor laws and the pass laws) had such a deep negative impact on the personal and professional lives of all black artists.

Listening to so many tales of struggle and tribulation, I kept needing to ask, why do it? Why be a singer against all these odds? Is it really worth it? Time and again the answer came back: I sang for the love of it. And yes, given a second chance, I'd do the same all over again.

LARA ALLEN
Cambridge, June 1997

FOOTNOTES

1 I gratefully acknowlege the financial assistance of the Patrick and Margaret Flannagan Scholarship, the Elizabeth Allan Scholarship and the Cambridge Livingstone Trust towards the costs of this research.

2 Veit Erlmann, *African Stars: Studies in Black South African Performance*, Chicago: Chicago University Press, 1991, pp 46-48.

3 A selection of these recordings are available on *Caluza's Double Quartet*, Heritage, HTCD19, 1992. The women who went to London with Caluza's Double Quartet were Evelyn Caluza, Beatrice Sinaye Khuzwayo, Irene (Lindi) Msane, Mrs A Ndimande, and Thembani Ngcobo. (Erlman, *African Stars*, p 142.)

4 Recordings by Griffiths Motsieloa's Pitch Black Follies and other vaudeville companies, as well as by early jazz bands like the Merry Blackbirds and the Jazz Maniacs, are available on the cassette accompanying Christopher Ballantine's book *Marabi Nights: Early South African Jazz and Vaudeville*, Johannesburg: Ravan Press, 1993.

5 According to Margorie Pretorius, other members included Dorothy Kupe and Mary Ramushu. (Margorie Pretorius. Interviewed by Lara Allen, Soweto, 18.4.96.) Lindi Makhanya, however, also remembers the participation at various times of Diana Marta, Ruth Mafuko, Netty Nkosi, Helena Dungwa, Peggy Bhengu and child stars Doris Shuping, Joyce Ndabane and Hilda Palmer. (Lindy Makhanya. Interviewed by Christopher Ballantine with Veit Erlmann, Soweto, 13.2.87.)

6 Ballantine, *Marabi Nights*, p 47-50.

7 *Zonk!* May 1956.

8 Some of the other singers who performed with the Synco Fans during the fifties were Hilda Seeku, Betty Naia, Ellen Mazibuko, Pamela Moloi, Paulina Puti, Maxine and Ursula Sentso, Violet Peterson and Ursula Bergman.

9 The Gay Gaieties took part in the first of Alfred Herbert's *African Jazz and Variety* shows, which took place in June 1954. (Bantu World, 19.6.54.)

10 Tandie sings her story on *Together as One, Music for Africa,* CDMFA 48, 1997.

11 Many recent publications celebrate the achievements of *Drum* and make selections of its contents available. *A Good-Looking Corpse* is a very readable, upbeat evocation of *Drum* during the fifties. (Mike Nicol, *A Good Looking Corpse*. London: Minerva, 1995.) *The "Drum" Decade* is one of best selections of *Drum* short stories and it includes an informative introductory essay by Michael Chapman. (Michael Chapman, ed. *The "Drum" Decade: Stories from the 1950s*. Pietermaritzburg: University of Natal Press, 1989.) The collected works of many *Drum* journalists have been published, for example William

"Bloke" Modisane, *Blame Me on History*. Johannesburg: Skotaville, 1987; Casey "Kid" Motsisi, *Casey & Co.: Collected Writings of Casey "Kid" Motsisi*. Muthobi Mutloatse (ed.). Johannesburg: Ravan Press, 1978; Todd Matshikiza, *Chocolates for my Wife*. Cape Town: Africasouth Paperbacks, 1982. There are also several books which feature glossy reproductions of *Drum* photographs, for example Jurgen Schadeberg (ed.). *The Fifties People of South Africa*. Johannesburg: Bailey's African Photo Archives, 1987.)

12 For example: *A Call for Peace*, The Elite Swingsters and Dolly Rathebe, Gallo Music Publishers, CDGMP F 40320, 1993; and *Siya Gida*, The Elite Swingsters and Dolly Rathebe, Teal Records, TELCD 2570, 1995. Some of Dolly's early recordings are available on *Township Swing Jazz! Volume 1*, Gallo Music Productions, CDZAC 53, 1991.

13 A good selection of Dorothy's fifties recordings have been reissued on *Hamba Notsokolo and Other Original Hits from the 50s*. Gallo Music Productions, CDZAC 60.

14 Rob Allingham. Sleeve notes accompanying *Hamba Notsokolo*. According to Allingham, some of the other singers who recorded at Troubadour during the fifties were Doris and Ruth Molifi, Harriet Oliphant, Ann Gxasheka, Lindi Khumalo, Dixie Kwankwa, Ida Sangwe and Orienta Mnkahla.

15 "Meadowlands" has been reissued on *From Marabi to Disco: 42 Years of Township Music*. Gallo Music Productions, CDZAC 61, 1994. This CD is an excellent compilation of South African historical recordings and includes many of the singers featured in this book.

16 Tandie Klaasen. Interviewed by Lara Allen, Johannesburg, 26.2.96.

17 Rob Allingham. Sleeve notes accompanying *Miriam Makeba and the Skylarks Volumes 1 and 2*, Teal Records, TELCD 2303 and TELCD 2315, 1991.

18 See *Miriam Makeba and the Skylarks Volume 1*, track 15.

19 Abigail Kubeka. Interviewed by Lara Allen, Johannesburg, 8.2.96.

20 David Coplan. *In Township Tonight!: South Africa's Black City Music and Theatre*. Johannesburg: Ravan Press, 1985, pp 150-151.

21 Dolly Rathebe. Interviewed by Lara Allen, Mabopane, 14.2.96.

22 Since the late eighties, music administrator and show promoter Queeneth Ndaba has been working through the Dorkay House Trust to restore this venue to its former glory.

23 A recording of the South African version of *King Kong* is available on *King Kong: Original Cast*, Gallo Music Productions, 66890-2.

24 The remaining female principals were Helen Gama, Ruth Nkonyeni, Phyllis Mqomo, Desirée Mkele and Esme Raborethi. Other members of the sixty-nine-strong cast included: Abigail Kubeka, Hazel Futa, Susan Gabashane, Mabel Mafuya, Mary Thobei, Thandeka Mpambane, Letta Mbulu, Tandie Kumalo, Linda Mhlongo, Marjorie Jordan, Dorothy Dube, Joyce Mdakane and Pricilla Booi.

25 The other female principals were Patience Gcwabe, Phyllis Mqomo, Tandie Kumalo, Louisa Emmanuel, Mabel Mafuya, Abigail Kubeka, Hazel Futa, Vinah Bendile and Martha Mdenge. Remaining members of the London cast included Ruth Nkonyeni, Tandie Klaasen, Rose Hlela, Priscilla Booi, Thandeka Mpambani, Linda Mhlongo, Mary Rabotapi, Letta Mbulu, Petunia Vika, Doris Kumalo and beauty queens Mimmie Edwards and Mamsie Mthombeni.

26 Classic recordings by Letta Mbulu recently released on CD include: *In the Music the Village Never Ends*, Sony Music, CDCOL 8015 P, 1996; *The Best of Letta and Caiphus*, Sony Music, CDCOL 8008 P, 1996; and *Naturally Letta Mbulu*, CCP Record Company, CDFAT (WM) 88, 1997.

27 Zakithi Dlamini. Interviewed by Lara Allen, Johannesburg, 28.8.95.

28 The 1983 recording of *Poppie Nongena* has been reissued on CD: *Poppie Nongena: Original Cast*, Rykodisc, HNCD 1351, 1983.

29 Some of the other singers who at various times recorded for the Dark City Sisters were Susan Gabashane: Francisca Mgomezulu, Ethel Mgomezulu, Dorothy Sosibo, Bessie Tshabalala, Irene Mawela, Nunu Maseko, Kate Oleni, Thoko Khumalo and Emma Seneke.

30 Many of the best Dark City Sisters recordings are available on *Dark City Sisters and Flying Jazz Queens*, Earthworks, CDEWV 31, 1993; and *Best of Dark City Sisters*, CCP Record Company, CDCCP (WP) 1119, 1997.

31 Some recent recordings by this ensemble are: *The Best of Mahlatini and the Mahotella Queens*, Gallo Music Publishers, CDHUL 40274; *Women of the World*, Gallo Music Publishers, CD GMP 40331; and *Paris-Soweto*, Mahlatini and the Mahotella Queens, Gallo Music Publishers, CD GMP 40314.

32 The better-known group was Hilda Tloubatla, Nobesuthu Shawe and Mildred Mangxola, who sing with Mahlatini. The other group consisted of Beatrice Ngcobo, Emily Zwane and Caroline Karpenta.

33 Singers who have recorded as the Mahotella Queens since 1969 include: Emily Zwane, Olive Masinga, Thandi Radebe, Thandi Kheswa, Thandi Nkosi, Caroline Karpentar, Beatrice Ngcobo, Irene Mawela and Hazel Zwane.

34 A selection of Margaret Singana's hits are available on CD: *Lady Africa*, Gallo Music Publishers, CDRED 603, 1997.

35 Available on *The Best of Brenda and the Big Dudes*, CCP Record Company, CDBREN (WR) 001, 1993, track 1.

36 Available on *The Best of Yvonne Chaka Chaka*, Teal Records, CDRBL 190, track 2.

37 A selection of Rebecca's gospel hits are available on *Free at Last*, Hemisphere, 7243 8 5712722, 1997.

38 *Babhemu*, Busi Mhlongo & Twasa. BMG Records, CDBSP (WL) 2044, 1994.

39 *Ancient Evenings*, Sibongile Khumalo, Sony Music, CDCOL 8001 P, 1996; and *Inyakanyaka*, Tu Nokwe, Teal Records, CDRBL 247, 1996.

40 Ballantine, *Marabi Nights*, p 47.

41 Nothembi's most recent release is *Vukani Bomma*, RPM Record Company, CDAFR 139, 1995.

Abigail Kubeka

Grim, unwavering determination to become a singer marked Abigail Kubeka in her teens, but the realisation of her dream would not come easily.

She had to pay a high price. Her mother desperately wanted her daughter to become a nurse, and chased Abigail away from home when she insisted on pursuing a singing career instead. The result was that the stary-eyed and ambitious Abigail went to stay at Mofolo Village, Soweto, with Miriam Makeba, who had offered her accommodation.

Abigail was fortunate. She joined one of the top groups of the fifties, the Skylarks, an all-female group under the leadership of Miriam – so her progress and increasing earning power were steady. This enabled her to stick to a cast-iron rule that she would take all the money she made back home to her mother. Even so, her mother still disapproved.

"But it's a different story when I visit her now," Abigail laughs mischievously when she recalls her mother's initial refusal to accept her career.

Today, after an amazing career that has taken her right to the top, Abigail quite understands her mother's apprehension. If you were young, African and educated in the fifties, you had to become a nurse or a teacher or, if your family's finances and luck would allow it, a medical doctor or lawyer. Less fortunate girls were swallowed up by the factories in the city, domestic service in the white suburbia of apartheid South Africa or early marriage.

Not Abigail. Inspired by popular musicians of the time, like the Manhattan Brothers, the African Inkspots, the Woody Woodpeckers and "the Emily Kwenanes, Dolly Rathebes, Thoko Thomos and Mabel Magadas", she was adamant to make it on the stage.

She takes up the story: "At a concert in Kilnerton in the late forties, a guy named Vandi Leballo heard me sing. He was bowled over and, without wasting any time, arranged that I work with the Huddleston Jazz Band (named after Father Trevor Huddleston, whose encouragement led to the formation of the band). It was a good match, because I was the same age as Hugh Masekela and Jonas Gwangwa and most of the other band members. I was the band's vocalist and worked with them during school vacations. Then there was a show at Johannesburg's Bantu Men's Social Centre where the band shared the stage with the Manhattan Brothers. Miriam (Makeba) was invited to listen and she was impressed by me. After the show she invited me to join her group, the Skylarks."

That is when Abigail moved to Mofolo village and became member of this celebrated group, consisting of Mary Rabotapi, Helen van Rensberg and Mummy Girl Nketle, with Miriam Makeba as their leader. Sometimes Nomonde Sihawu joined them, as did Sam Ngakane, who added some spice and depth with his singing bass.

The Skylarks broke new ground with their truly unique music, a mix of contemporary Western pop and indigenous sounds. By 1958 they were the hottest musical group in South Africa, with hits like "Hush", "Uyadela" and "Hamba Bhekile". They were at the right place at the right time. Inspired by the great American all-women and black groups like the McGuire Sisters, and the earlier Boswell Sisters and Andrews Sisters of the 1930s and 1940s, they fitted in with the prevailing musical taste, especially in the African townships.

Abigail tells of her career in show business: "After the Skylarks era, it was *King Kong* for me. I won a part in it as one of Miriam's shebeen girls."

You touch a raw nerve when you ask about the forces that shaped her as a singer: her struggles as a woman in a male-dominated domain; a world fraught with danger in crime-ridden African communities where female singers were seen as easy prey for gangsters and, of course, the low status accorded to a career in music in her need-driven society.

"I feel I have been through the mill. It's the love I received from my people, the audiences, that kept me going. That sustained me. There were the rough patches, of course. Like when we were not allowed to sing in white clubs in the cities, but all those experiences gave me strength. It was my way of fighting the political battle for my people.

"I know suffering, I know pain. My message is always in my music. The first person that influenced me in my music was Dolly Rathebe. I loved that sisi (sister).

"There was also Miriam Makeba, who I admired – and still admire – for her discipline. She taught me a lot when I was under her wing. Those two ladies, Dolly and Miriam, are so different and I was lucky to have picked up something from each of them. That is what made me what I am today. They are two great women, who are different and talented."

Jazz has always been a trademark of Abigail's work, and she agrees without hesitation that she is essentially a jazz singer. She attributes this to the era in South African music when she made her breakthrough with the Skylarks.

This was later re-enforced by the late Sarah "Sassy" Vaughan. The two women met while Sarah was on tour in Lesotho. They clicked immediately and shared trade secrets.

Abigail believes that the big time is at hand in South Africa.

"Now is the time to take off. Opportunities are opening up." Her features harden to show the determination that started her off as a teenager and took her to the top in one of the toughest jobs in town.

Today, after 36 years in show business, in a career that has made her a household name in the South African cabaret, stage and screen world and that has taken her to England, Germany, Zimbabwe, Malawi and Mozambique, Abigail will tell you: "If I could live my life over, I would do it all again and become a singer. But this time I would start as a sixteen-year-old, hopefully with knowledge and experience."

Interviewed at her home in Orlando West in Soweto in 1993

Anneline Malebu

It was in Guguletu township outside Cape Town that Anneline Malebu made a dramatic decision to become a singer. When her mother heard about it she took her to the local police station where she wanted the police to knock some sense into her.

But the unshakable Anneline had made her decision.

"I had big dreams. I saw myself becoming a famous singer and, through music, going far away from home. This distracted me and I was not concentrating on my studies," she recalls.

Then one day, when Anneline was in standard seven, something inside her snapped. She stood up in class, took all her books and started giving them away to fellow classmates. In a determined voice she announced that she was through with school and wanted to be a singer.

She remembers that year, 1970, as the turning point in her life.

"Mom was hurt. She wanted the police to convince me that school was best for me. The matter finally ended up in the Children's Court, and they told my mother to give me a chance. She reluctantly agreed, but she was visibly hurt."

Anneline threw herself body and soul into a show-business career, starting with the Flamingoes, a local group that gave her a taste of things to come.

She later joined Joy, a chart-busting all-women group. By 1979 they had thousands of fans eating out of their hands. That year Joy made history by becoming the first black group to break through the colour barrier of the SABC (South African Broadcasting Corporation) annual music awards, which up till then had been organised along segregated lines. Joy won every category in the awards – best album, best-produced single (for their amazing hit "Paradise Road"), best producer and best songwriter. During the awards ceremony Joy was showered with accolades.

"That night my mother, whom I had invited to the awards night, couldn't believe what she saw and heard. It was too much for her and she silently disappeared from

the theatre and went outside into the night. She sat on the pavement and wept."

Anneline's voice chokes a little as she recalls that night.

"Later, when I found her sitting there, she reminded me of that day she took me to the police station. She apologised for ever doubting me. We went back into the theatre and enjoyed ourselves."

Anneline's musical leanings have always been towards jazz. She cites among her early influences people like Winston "Mankunku" Ngozi, one of South Africa's top jazzmen, and a host of others who were always around during her formative years in Guguletu. Her family had moved there from Athlone, where she was born.

"There was also the garbage-collector gentleman who, during his rounds in our street in Guguletu, would sing some of the most incredible jazz tunes. I also listened a lot to American singers like Mahalia Jackson, Chaka Khan, Millie Jackson and the Staple Singers."

While struggling as an unknown in the early 1970s, she had a lucky break: she took part in a tour that included top names Jonathan Butler and Lionel Peterson. When the show ended in Johannesburg, Anneline did not return to Cape Town – thanks to another singer, Babsy Mlangeni, who made it all happen for her when he introduced her to the manager of The Pelican, at that stage one of the trendiest clubs in Soweto.

"This gave me the opportunity to play with some of the great musicians of the time," recalls Anneline, "and I made my name and became a very big star. That is where I was spotted by the Tshabalala family, who were funding the show and who offered me a supporting act in the Staple Singers tour of South Africa that they were putting together.

"The owner of the club was taken by surprise on my opening night. He could not believe what he heard. The audience went wild. They were all jumping from their seats. I was immediately offered a permanent spot on the club's cabaret list."

With her performance during the sell-out Staple Singers tour, Anneline's place among top African singers was assured. When she, Felicia Marion and Thoko Ndlozi formed the trio Joy in 1975 on her return to Johannesburg, there was no looking back for the girl from Guguletu.

When Joy disbanded two years later, Anneline formed another exciting but short-lived all-female group, Shadiii, with promising newcomers Tsidii Le Loka and Faith Kekana. "By forming Shadiii," Anneline says, "I was trying to wipe the tears from the faces of the Joy fans."

Anneline disappeared from the show-business scene for some time in the late seventies and hid in Lesotho, where she quietly worked in a band with her cousin. In 1989 she was off to the United States to join the acclaimed *Sheila's Day*, a musical put up by South African exiles.

After touring some major cities in the US and Canada, Anneline returned to South Africa and was back at Johannesburg's Civic Theater, the site of her greatest triumph in 1979 when Joy walked off with all the SABC music awards – but this time appearing in Mbongeni Ngema's 1993 musical *Magic at 4 a.m.*

Anneline has not forgotten the people in South Africa who helped to make her dream of being a musician come true.

Interviewed at the Civic Theatre, Johannesburg, in 1993

Brenda Fassie

In a stormy music career of over twenty years, volumes have already been written about this controversial singer. Boasting a jazz singer's voice, but a taste for greater fame and riches than that offered by that style, many believe Brenda Fassie has the potential for international stardom.

Her career has been built on a combination of incredible self-confidence, real talent and a highly-charged sexual persona. A key to her success appears to be her dynamic stage presence.

She once told a writer from *Cosmopolitan* magazine that she was too good to be in the middle of the magazine. "I belong on the front because I am best. Musically, sexually, I'm the best."

That is Brenda Fassie, the red-hot pop dynamo. Her recording company, CCP, referring to her eleventh album *I'm Not a Bad Girl*, believes that she is the most successful female recording artist yet to come from South Africa: she has sold more than a million records in less than ten years.

It has been a bumpy ride for the Cape Town-born Brenda, who took her first step towards bright lights, fame and fortune in 1979. That was when well-known record producer Koloi Lebona asked her mother's permission to take her to Johannesburg.

Brenda was not well known outside the black music circles in her native Cape Town, but she was well trained: she was a seasoned pre-teen lead singer for the Cosmos, an Elsies River group, when Lebona spotted her. On arrival in Johannesburg, she joined the stable of the father of South African musical theatre, Gibson Kente.

Afterwards, she joined Papa and Blondie Makhene, the top Johannesburg band of the time, as a backing singer. It was a time of change for the band and it needed an identity in the pop market, which was expanding rapidly. This led to the birth of the Big Dudes in 1983, with Brenda as lead vocalist.

In no time Brenda and the Big Dudes cut a hit, "Weekend Special", which sold more than 20 000 copies within a month. And soon they produced hit after hit and sold more than 500 000 copies of their records – then equivalent of nine platinum discs.

"Weekend Special" unleashed a new vibe in the South African music industry and gave Brenda a strong following throughout the country.

She remembers those early years in Johannesburg when fame and fortune beckoned. "From 'Weekend Special' I was made. I was so ugly. I didn't have teeth. I remember (journalist) Jani Allen wrote an article about me and said that I looked like a horse."

Brenda became a self-made stylist who decided what she would wear on stage, and she worked out her dance routines in front of an enormous mirror in her bedroom.

When she stepped out of South Africa in 1992, she conquered all before her: 80 000 music lovers packed Zambia's Independence Stadium to hear her in a concert to raise funds for drought relief.

The same year, the BBC made a documentary about pop culture in South Africa and Brenda was featured prominently. The title of the documentary, "Not a Bad Girl", was taken from her 1991 hit album.

Controversy dogs Brenda. 1993 dealt her a particularly bad hand. She was arrested for bad debts and spent several hours at the Johannesburg Prison before being allowed out on bail. A year later she said in an interview with the Johannesburg *Sunday Times*: "I've been through a miserable time. It's the price of fame, I suppose. I've come through a rehabilitation programme and I'm straight."

What she meant was that she had come back from the brink, having fought and won a battle against cocaine addiction.

She was back in the headlines in 1995 when her 21-year-old companion, Poppie Sihlahla, apparently died of substance overdose in a room they shared at Johannesburg's Quirinale Hotel in Hillbrow. Brenda was finally taken by Gauteng premier Tokyo Sexwale, an outspoken fighter against drugs, and Brenda's old friend and fellow musician, Chicco

Twala, to a rehabilitation centre. In a *Drum* magazine story Brenda later explained that she was depressed in 1992 when her boyfriend did not give her a Valentine Day present. "He didn't even bring me a flower," she said.

But worse was to happen that day. Somebody offered her cocaine, and Brenda, low and dejected, accepted. It was her first taste of the drug but it put her on the road to disaster. Since then Brenda's life and career has been a see-saw. She was named Best Female Vocalist of 1995 in the All Africa Music Awards, and has recorded with Papa Wembe, one of Africa's most popular artists. Another record album, *It's my Time*, was released in December 1996. The album soon sold more than 25 000 copies to earn the gold disc status.

Early in 1997 Brenda was in the news again, this time the victim of a cruel magazine hatchet job. A newly-launched Johannesburg arts magazine, *eVibe*, plagiarised a *Newsweek* story on Madonna. The local magazine simply substituted the name "Madonna" with "Brenda".

It is ironic that Brenda would be compared to Madonna, because American journalist Donald G McNeil Jnr, writing for the *Star* in Johannesburg just a few weeks earlier, noted: "In interviews, the comparison to Madonna seems ridiculous. Madonna is a study in calculation; Fassie is all impulse. She cannot sit still, leaps to answer phones that aren't even hers, preemptorily sends people out for things like artificial fingernails and ice cream bars. She brags that she'll tell anybody who her sexual partner was the previous night."

Some people have called Brenda a braggart, others an oversexed, loud-mouthed wench. Perhaps *City Press* comes closest to the truth when it wrote, after a 1994 concert at Swaziland's International Trade Fair in Manzini: "Millions of people are totally absorbed in the lurid details of her private life, which is inevitable due to her high media profile, instead of focusing on her artistry, talent and stunning stage craft."

Brenda's performance, the newspaper continued, "confirmed that she is the hottest live performer in this country today…"

Compiled from published sources, 1997

Busi (Viccie) Mhlongo

Busi Mhlongo started to make her mark in the sixties, when jazz was probably the most popular music among urban blacks in South Africa.

By 1988 she was riding the crest of the wave in Holland after a six-week tour with her South African band, Twasa. Dutch music lovers were beside themselves, heaping praise on Busi and her band.

Her homecoming in 1993, after twenty years of working abroad, was painful.

"I think I'm somebody who has died in this country. I mean, nobody knows about me. But I have this consolation that if I'm not known in my country, I'm a South African in Holland. People there appreciate what I do."

There is sadness in her voice as she shows you a pile of clippings from Dutch newspapers. One of the clippings contains a touching paragraph by critic Jacob Haagsma: "Sometimes it is difficult to understand that a country so overtaken by violence can produce such beautiful music. South Africa at the moment may not be the most homely place, but the songs of Busi Mhlongo are not any less sparkling for it."

The road has been long and hard for Durban-born Busi, who was inspired when she saw a teenage Letta Mbulu performing in the Durban City Hall in 1959.

"I saw Letta in *King Kong* and had to convince my mom that I also wanted to be a singer like Letta. *King Kong* changed a lot of things for me and my contemporaries in Durban," says Busi who, as a schoolgirl at the famed Natal's Ohlange High School, loved every note and harmony in the songs of top African groups of the time – the Manhattan Brothers, the African Inkspots and the Skylarks.

"At home they used to buy a lot of records. I would sneak out, leaving my household chores, and go to the back of our house and listen to the music through the window. For me it was Dorothy Masuka, Miriam Makeba and Letta Mbulu. They sort of convinced me that I could make it as a musician."

Busi and her coevals Doreen Webster, Ndaba Mhlongo and Simon Sabela got the opportunity they had been waiting for when they were recruited by talent scout Sam Alcock to join his studio in Johannes-

burg, "because there was a void after *King Kong* had left on a tour of England."

Competition was stiff, but Busi cleared her throat and got on with the apprenticeship, working and recording with a number of musicians. Some of the groups with whom she worked under different labels and formats included the Durbanites and the Gallo Kids.

"But maybe the big break for me came in 1964 when I joined Early Mabuza at Dorkay House (where Union Artists was based). That is where I met music giants like Gibson Kente. In fact, I later joined Kente's musical *Manana the Jazz Prophet*. Dorkay House was like home. There were so many good musicians."

Many a jazz lover will cherish the memory of a bitterly cold Saturday afternoon in 1964 at Soweto's Orlando Stadium. On that occasion Busi took South African jazz to dizzy heights with the Early Mabuza Septet and a star-studded 25-piece all-African big band under the leadership of composer-pianist Gideon Nxumalo. The South Africans played a visiting American trio, led by pianist George "Stardust" Green, with LaVern Baker as their vocalist, under the table.

There is a common misconception that it was her late husband, Early Mabuza, one of South Africa's finest modern jazz drummers, who first got Busi to work as a serious jazz artist. She concedes that Mabuza was a great influence, but she says, "It was Ndaba Mhlongo who got me into jazz."

From there until 1968, no jazz show was complete without Busi. But things changed unexpectedly. She left for Lourenço Marques (now Maputo) in neighbouring Mozambique with the revue *African Jazz*, not knowing that she would not see her native land for another twenty years. After

finishing the Maputo gig, she went directly to Portugal.

"And, next thing, Early was dead. I was hardly gone a year." After her musician husband's sudden death of natural causes, she continued working overseas in London and the United States, and much later in Holland.

Since returning home she has been going great guns. She has performed in select stage shows and appeared on television. In 1995 a local record company, Sheer Sound, was licensed by her Dutch record company to distribute her music in South Africa, especially her best-selling 1994 debut album *Ababhemu*, which was recorded in Belgium. Said Damon Frobed, founder of Sheer Sound, an independent South African recording company: "I definitely believe that I have taken the best decision by signing on Busi to be my first indigenous artist. She is going places and very soon the country will begin to appreciate how fortunate we are to have been blessed by a talented singer who upholds African culture and has given her life to music."

Busi was on the headline bill of the mainstream music programme at the 1995 National Arts Festival in Grahamstown, where she appeared with widely known South African musician Sipho Gumede. Since then Busi has been performing in a number of concerts, especially at the Durban Playhouse, currently the premier venue in KwaZulu-Natal.

In 1996 she performed at a sold-out concert in Johannesburg where she shared the stage with Nothembi Mkhwebane, the queen of Ndebele music. Still Busi considers her 1964 Orlando Stadium performance and the popular mid-sixties Saturday afternoon jazz gigs at the Johannesburg Planet Hotel special triumphs in her long career.

You would think that after all the years in show business Busi would have no fears about the stage, yet she admits that she suffers stage fright the minute she approaches the microphone to sing.

"It's like an inner voice telling me that if I don't make it in my first number, I'm not going to make it at all."

No one in the audience would ever suspect that fear.

Interviewed at Johnnesburg International (then Jan Smuts) Airport, 1993

Dark City Sisters

Way back in 1956 when an excited Grace Msika (Moeketsi) handed her mother the eight pounds she had received for a recording, there was disappointment waiting for her.

Her suspicious, no-nonsense washerwoman mother refused point-blank to accept the money. Nor did she want it in her house. Instead she demanded to know where her teenage daughter had got the money. Did she steal it? How on earth could a girl so young earn so much money?

Grace had to do some quick thinking. First she hid the "tainted" money in their yard in New Look location (later Dlamini township in Soweto). The following day she went back to Johannesburg to Teal Records, then a licencee of the famous RCA, and asked for a letter confirming that she had indeed recorded the single. In addition to the letter, Teal gave her a copy of the recording. These were sufficient proof for her mother.

"It was then she believed me. After that incident she opened up and accepted my career as a singer," says Grace, who at the time was singing under her maiden name of Grace Msika with the Sunbeams, who boasted an impressive line-up of Miriam Makeba, Mary Rabotapi and Johanna Radebe, but with whom she never made a record.

Grace started singing in the Apostolic Church choir in Sophiatown, but her 1956 record with Teal set her on the road to a hectic show-business career.

In 1960 she was approached by Rupert Bopape, a prominent talent scout for EMI, to join the high-riding mbaqanga group Dark City Sisters, which was initially an all-women studio singing group. The group's name derived from the fact that most members hailed from the notorious Alexandra township, east of Johannesburg, which was then commonly known as the "Dark City".

At the time, the Dark City Sisters comprised Francisca Mngomezulu, Esther Khoza, Hilda Moghapi, Joyce Mogatusi, Ethel Mngomezulu, Joyce Seneke, Thoko Khumalo and Thoko Dube.

"At that time mbaqanga music was the flavour of the moment," Grace recalls. "And to be invited to join a top group like the Dark City Sisters was indeed an honour for a musician."

Their ace backing band was made up of, among others, the late Zacks Nkosi and Shadrack Piliso, and Ntemi Piliso, today one of South Africa's oldest active musicians.

"There were also our music teachers, like Ellison Themba, Michael Xaba, Roland Mqebu and Elijah Nkwanyane. They were a down-to-earth outfit that made us sweat blood when they took us through our tonic-solfa music lessons," Grace recalls.

Mondays to Fridays were taken up by music lessons and recording sessions in a punishing schedule; weekends the sisters took off. Sometimes, there would be an occasional show in the then Northern Transvaal (now Northern Province), organised by Bopape.

But this Monday-to-Friday arrangement did not satisfy the artistic hunger of the Dark City Sisters, so they met secretly at weekends to stage shows at venues in Standerton, Sasolburg, Welkom, Bloemfontein and Pretoria.

Then one day one of the band members blew the whistle on them. After a tongue-lashing from Bopape, he eventually allowed the Sisters to spread their wings, becoming extremely popular in places like Durban, Port Elizabeth and beyond South Africa's borders in what are now Zimbabwe, Botswana and Zambia.

But by 1968 the writing was on the wall for mbaqanga music. It was gradually losing its appeal. Disco was pushing mbaqanga aside in townships all over South Africa.

"After a tour to Cape Town and Rhodesia (Zimbabwe) we disbanded the group. There was no point in going on. Disco music was the 'in' thing." Grace's voice and eyes betray obvious nostalgia.

Joyce Seneke, Esther Khoza and Francesca Mngomezulu, members of the original Dark City Sisters, have passed away, and except for Joyce Mogatusi, the whereabouts of the others is unknown. But there have been efforts to revive the Dark City Sisters. In 1994 Tusk came out with the album *The Return of the Dark City Sisters*. Two other mbaganga vocalists were featured with Grace and Joyce in this venture, which did not sell very well.

Grace, now 61, remembers their heyday: "We composed our own music, and it was based on daily events, incidents and happenings around us. We would work for something like a week on a given composition. Gifted people like guitarist Almon Memela would always be there to help us out, especially the music part of the story we were putting across."

Grace's main musical influence was Dolly Rathebe: "Especially her hit 'Unozizwe'. I wanted to be like her. Sing like her. She was all that was good and beautiful in music for me," she laughs.

She also counts the Quad Sisters under Tandie Klaasen (then Mpambani), Nancy Jacobs (of the mid-fifties hit song "Meadowlands") and the Leeuw Sisters as major influences in her career.

Of course, like a legion of her contemporaries, there is the obligatory American influence. For Grace it was Ella Fitzgerald, organist Jimmy Smith and gospel-music diva Mahalia Jackson.

Discipline, Grace emphasises, is the glue that kept the Dark City Sisters together and made them such a top-class act.

"We had disciplined ourselves that we would become the greatest female singing group in South Africa," she says. "Maybe we achieved that status. Time will tell."

Grace Moeketsi interviewed at her home in Pimville, Soweto, in 1997

Joyce Mogatusi

Dolly Rathebe

She has graced the covers of the mass-circulation African magazines *Drum* and *Zonk!* She has entertained and inspired audiences and fellow musicians for more than forty years. Her lovely face and dazzling smile are instantly recognisable from countless advertisements for skin-lightening creams, floor polish and beauty soaps. Yet she often had to sleep in shebeens because there was no other place where a African woman singer was welcome.

She is Dolly Rathebe, and her story begins in 1949 as a carefree young Sophiatown girl who had many things going for her: a lovely singing voice, a lively social life and a reckless spirit of youth that mirrored her times, the roaring fifties – epitomised by American fashion and music.

This was particularly the case in Sophiatown, the melting pot of an emerging urban South African culture that bordered on the bohemian.

"I loved to sing at school, parties and everywhere. Then I heard some people were looking for a leading lady to star in *Jim Comes to Jo'burg*. This was in 1949," says Dolly. Talent scout Sam Alcock approached her, and she agreed to go for auditions. She was destined to become South Africa's first African film star.

Dolly never looked back. She was introduced to the glamour and glitz of show business and she met, befriended and learnt a lot from early African women singers like Johanna Radebe, one of the big music "sisters" at the time.

By the early fifties Dolly stood unchallenged. The music-loving urban black audiences adored her. She treasures her memories of the countless shows at the Johannesburg City Hall with the sizzling *African Jazz and Variety* revue.

"I have always loved music, that has been my bread." Dolly flashes an attractive smile as she speaks of the force that has spotlighted her as the spirit of an age of great urban African music and culture.

It comes as no surprise when she says her main early influence was American Lena Horne, who with her 1940s film classics *Cabin in the Sky* and *Stormy Weather* had become the darling and symbol of pride and achievement among thousands of urban Africans in South Africa.

Dolly also counts Ella Fitzgerald and Dakota Staton among her influences. Locally, the "Empress of the Blues", Emily Kwenane, was her major inspiration.

"I loved that woman. She was powerful. We used to call her Ella (Fitzgerald)," Dolly says in her fresh mezzo voice.

Other inspirations for Dolly were local vocalists like the young Miriam Makeba and her contemporary, Tandie Mpambani (later Klaasen).

Although Dolly has not forgotten the hard times, and had to endure the problems and hardships that were part of a black woman singer's life in the fifties, she says that she and most of her contemporaries enjoyed what they were doing. "We never did it for money. There was also the wonderful spirit and cooperation among fellow musicians." She remembers how she hurriedly roped in top musicians like the late Skip Phahlane at the Johannesburg street corner popularly known as "Loafers' Corner" for the recording of "Sindi", one of her most memorable blues hits of the fifties.

"Sindi" has a wonderful history. It was originally played by a concertina troubadour, Siganada Cele, as "Good Street", dedicated to a notorious street of that name in Sophiatown. Almost at the same time that Dolly recorded the song as "Sindi", American jazzman Johnny Hodges recorded it under the title "Something to Put your Foot to".

Dolly's hit reached the US after American actor Sidney Poitier's visit to South Africa in 1949 for the filming of Alan Paton's *Cry, the Beloved Country*. Poitier, a saxophonist and flautist on the side, fell in love with the song and took it along to his homeland.

To the delight of Dolly's fans she re-recorded the song with the Elite Swingsters in 1991. It was released on the album *Woza!* Dolly also features on the Elite Swingsters' 1995 album *Siya Gida - We Dance*.

It is a happy colaboration, yet Dolly has not forgotten the musicians she worked with in the past. With a note of nostalgia she says: "I miss the boys that are late – Kippie Moeketsi, Mackay Davashe and Early Mabuza. I miss that crowd. Nowadays, it seems, most of our guys know only how to play mbaqanga. It's the 'in' thing. Those days musicians could read music."

Of the current crop of female African singers, Dolly simply says: "I am very proud of them. Especially Rebecca (Malope), who sings so well."

This is Dolly Rathebe, the woman who started her music career singing in churches, at weddings and later at wakes for dead family, relatives and friends.

Can Themba, doyen of African journalists, once wrote in *Drum* magazine that she went before her audiences "and treated them to live, wriggling flesh and she purred to them in a shaggy, hairy, deep, sultry mezzo. And she sang to them of the unachieved, half-realised longings of their own lives."

Dolly Rathebe, the woman who, after forty years in show business, has no regrets.

Interviewed at Dorkay House, Johannesburg, 1993

Dorothy Masuka

Dorothy Masuka passionately believes that singers, like good wine, mature with age. After more than forty years in show business she has mastered the technique of "playing around" with any song she chooses to sing.

"For instance," her eyes light up, "I can sing my hit 'Notsokolo' better than I did forty years ago. And I promise you, it's going to get even better."

She is concerned about women who are now starting out on their music careers. "If you have heard one, you have heard them all," she observes. She argues that musicians should start by examining what song is all about in the first place. To Dorothy, singing is about telling stories, talking about something or somebody your audience relates to.

"I think in most cases it's their music that prevents you from hearing what they are saying. You end up looking for something (meaningful) in their music. And in most cases I don't find that meaning, that message."

Dorothy believes that this has a lot to do with a singer's training and apprenticeship. Like many singers of the 1950s, she served her apprenticeship and received her training in the school of hard knocks.

Her songs like the hit "Ngimavuku-vuku" and "Umthetho Unzima" are eloquent testimony of that apprenticeship. "In those days we worked ourselves like mules. Every day of our singing lives you would swear that we were people doing regular day jobs. People like Mabel Mafuya can bear me out.

"What would happen is that a tune would come to me. Maybe it was inspired by our maskanda troubadours. We would then work on that tune until we got it right before recording."

Dorothy is convinced that modern technology in the recording industry has, to some extent, something to do with the declining standards of most singers nowadays.

"Today you are recording the voice, the following day it's the guitars. The recording studios are always fitting things and sounds into your song. Most of the time things that don't fit. Look at what is happening here in South Africa. People are no longer singing, they are bang-banging."

Dorothy, who first burst into the limelight in 1953 with "Into Yam", sees another potential danger facing African women singers. According to her, they are losing touch with their people's long tradition of song-making. As example, she mentions the Basotho street musicians who were so much a part of the South African urban black culture of the fifties. Talking about the African tradition of music-making, she argues that rap music is nothing but maskanda music that has been turned around and made to appear to have come from African-Americans.

The road Dorothy has travelled in her music career has been long and hard. She remembers when she started out in show business in her native country, the former Southern Rhodesian, now Zimbabwe.

"I won ten pounds at a beauty contest. But I had to tell the organisers that I could not accept it because my parents would kill me. They had to approach my parents first and explain everything. When the organisers left my home, I got a beating, just to teach me that my parents were against a stage career for me," Dorothy laughs as she recalls the incident.

She moved to South Africa, and it was while attending Johannesburg's St Thomas School as a bright-eyed ten-year-old that she became aware of her voice and ability to sing. She enjoyed listening to American singers like Ella Fitzgerald, Sarah Vaughan and Mahalia Jackson.

It was in 1950 or '51 when she was discovered in Pimville township by Troubadour Records. Suddenly she entered the world of top vocalists like Dolly Rathebe, Miriam Makeba, Mabel Mafuya, Mary Thobei and Nancy Jacobs.

It was only a matter of time before Dorothy joined the great testing ground and showcase of African talent of the day, Alf Herbert's *African Jazz and Variety*. This revue represented the best of African singing – male and female – and she pitted herself against names like Sonny Pillay and Ben "Satch" Masinga.

By 1955 African music lovers were raving about Dorothy Masuka, and she appeared on the covers of the mass-circulation African magazines *Drum* and *Zonk!*

Dorothy looks back on her career in South Africa, particularly in the fifties, and smiles: "I was powerful from the word go. I remember a tour with the Harlem Swingsters when we were promoting my hit 'Notsokolo'. I was a young woman among experienced musicians like Ben 'Gwigwi' Mrwebi, Dolly Rathebe and Mackay Davashe."

But then came 1960, a painful year that threatened to end her career. Because of the apartheid laws, she could only perform for designated African audiences in designated venues. She decided to leave South Africa for a while. To her shock, she discovered that she would not be allowed to return.

"I didn't do anything wrong. I was just singing some messages to the people, but I suppose the messages were not what some other people wanted to hear me sing. And they wouldn't give me a visa to return to my country."

As an exile, she worked on the cabaret circuit in London, Paris, Rome, Berlin, Tanzania, Malawi, Uganda and Zimbabwe, where she honed her skills while winning acclaim.

Dorothy has that unusual ability to get behind her music, a phrase, and make it connect with her audience.

What has made her one of the greatest singers produced in South Africa? Letta Mbulu got to the heart of the matter when she said in an earlier interview with the author: "She (Dorothy) was my love because she was an innovator. When she recorded, her music was so different and fresh."

Interviewed at Dorkay House, Johannesburg, 1993

Eaglet Ditse

Eaglet Ditse grew up with music around her. Her father, Alfred Nthodi, was an accomplished musician who had made a name as a singer and accordion player, in the style of a township troubadour, in Newclare, the "mixed" Johannesburg suburb where Eaglet was born. Her father was nicknamed "King of the Russians" because he was a Basotho, and in those days Basotho men were known as the "Russians".

"I used to go around Newclare streets with him, singing and collecting the money that appreciative residents showered on us," says Eaglet.

There was always music in their house. Eaglet remembers hiding under the dining-room table when Miriam Makeba and her Skylarks rehearsed at their house in Orlando West later. She would listen to the musicians hammering out their tunes and giving shape and form to their songs.

"When Miriam got her break and went overseas, she wanted to take me along," Eaglet recalls. That was in 1959, and her mother refused because she was the only child at her home. "But," she adds, "because of my association with Miriam Makeba, when I went to high school, my teachers noticed that I had a good singing voice."

Soweto's Orlando West High School played an important role in Eaglet's development as a musician. It was there, too, that a group of talented fellow students, among others Sipho "Hotstix" Mabuse and Alec "Om" Khoali, decided to form the Beaters. The group went on to win popularity in the African townships of the late seventies. For a while, Eaglet sang for this top soul group.

In the early seventies, Soweto in particular was undergoing a music revolution that would affect the rest of the country. Along with the Beaters and the talented musician Mara Louw, Eaglet was convinced that her future lay in music.

But she did not rely only on her conviction and musical background. She was prepared to work hard, so she expanded her musical knowledge by joining the top choral Wilba Music Group, and enrolling at Johannesburg's Jubilee Centre for formal musical training.

By the time her parents sent her to the Thaba Nchu Teacher Training College in the former Orange Free State in 1977, Eaglet had already made her name as a singer of great promise and had "conquered" the booming Johannesburg night club circuit, with successful performances at Soweto's Pelican Club and The New York Club in Fordsburg.

"After I qualified as a teacher, I realised that music was the only career for me," laughs Eaglet.

Between 1981 and 1986 she worked with the SABC, doing gospel music, voice-overs and a number of related activities.

With pain, Eaglet remembers one show that revealed the power of music to her. She was performing at Atteridgeville outside Pretoria with jazzmen Winston "Mankunku" Ngozi and Stompie Manana, as well as Tandie Klaasen, who was making an appearance after an incident that left her face badly scarred.

"After I had finished my song, Tandie asked me, as she was going on stage, what song she must sing. Without much thought, I told her to sing 'The First Time I Saw Your Face'. To me that was symbolic, because it was the first time after her misfortune that I had met and performed with her."

Tandie Klaasen gave such a moving rendition of the song that most of the audience was in tears. When Eaglet realised what was happening, she broke down backstage.

These days, Eaglet says, she is taking it easy and giving her two children all the love, guidance and support they need. However, she hastens to add, she has neither retired nor faded from of the music scene. The time and attention she now lavishes on her children is her special way of making up for the hard growing-up years they had to spend with their grandmother while she was clawing her way up the musical ladder.

"I'm also looking at some work proposals from a Nigerian musician," says Eaglet, who lists Ella Fitzgerald, Shirley Brown, Shirley Bassey, Esther Phillips and Natalie Cole as her main music influences. But Ella holds a special place in her heart: "She inspired me to attend music school and have a deeper understanding of music."

Eaglet does not doubt that good black women singers in South Africa can make it anywhere, given a chance, but she pleads that South African show business needs a long-overdue spring-cleaning to get rid of the incompetence and general rot that is eating at its soul.

Hence she is quick to give a word of warning for aspiring singers. When she started out, there were instances in which she would find herself on tour with two other women in the company of more than thirty male musicians.

"In that situation the women singers understood only one thing: that they were on tour to work and nothing else. Promoters took a dim view of things like getting drunk on stage or coming late. The promoters docked hefty sums from your pay."

It has been a long and hard climb, but Eaglet never gave up.

Interviewed at her Soweto home, 1993

Felicia Marion

Twenty years ago Felicia was just an ordinary saleslady at a prominent Johannesburg departmental store. Few customers would have guessed that behind the calm exterior burnt a fierce ambition to make it as a singer, or that at night the young saleslady was doing cabaret at clubs in Bosmont, a so-called coloured suburb outside Johannesburg.

Felicia started singing at the age of nine when she used to perform with her father during annual body-building contests in Pietermaritzburg, KwaZulu-Natal, where she was born.

"Before that, of course, my stage was my parents' kitchen table," laughs Felicia, who at fourteen formed an all-girl group with her sister, who played bass. The other two girls played drums and the guitar.

The group lasted just under a year before it disbanded and Felicia left for Johannesburg to seek her fame and fortune as a singer.

In mid-1974 she graduated from Bosmont to The Pelican Club, Soweto's hottest music venue at the time, where many a music career was made. It was a tough testing ground where only the best could survive.

"I was there for eighteen months, every weekend. Then I went back home to Pietermaritzburg. I thought I had it all wrapped up," recalls Felicia.

When top musician Sammy Brown came to her hometown to scout for talent, Felicia's uncle made her audition. Brown was impressed. Shortly afterwards, Felicia was on her way back to Johannesburg, where she was plunged into a show, *Solo Flight*, with Mavis Maseko and Mandisa Naudie from Port Elizabeth.

The show was not a financial success and folded after three months. But in 1976 Des and Dawn Lindberg, the well-known show-business impresario team, came onto the scene, looking for artists for their production of *The Black Mikado*.

"After two auditions, which didn't work out, Des and Dawn thought there was something in me they wanted to bring out. They asked me to do a private audition at their house, and I got a part in one of the choruses." Felicia was to work in the show until October 1976.

For the rest of the year she worked as a soloist for Spirits Rejoice, one of the best bands at the time. Gradually she was gaining experience and exposure. But her time had not yet come.

In 1977 matters changed for the better. With Anneline Malebu and Thoko Ndlozi, Felicia formed Joy, soon to be one of the country's most successful all-women groups. The group was an instant success, and fans flocked in their hundreds to sold-out concerts country-wide.

One of their hits, "Paradise Road", was the crowning glory in an amazingly successful though short career.

Today Felicia explains why Joy was disbanded: "The group disbanded when I converted to Christianity in 1982. I had found that I was not comfortable with what I was doing. We (Joy) tried to train someone else (to replace me) before I left. But she had a problem. Then we agreed that instead of continuing with another member, because we were so unique, we had to call it quits."

Felicia believes that gospel music, which she now sings, is going to play a prominent part in South Africa in the future.

"Many people are scared to go to church and to listen to a pastor. When it comes to gospel music, people are more open to it. Because the message is so powerful and positive, it's going to draw a lot of people because there is nowhere else we can turn to now.

"Music, secular music, is fine, but it does not fill the deepest void in you. Gospel music goes deeper than emotions, it goes to the soul, to the spirit. That is why it is going to be prominent."

And this also explains what drives her as a musician. "As a musician I found that what affects us in our daily lives, and the people around us, can only come through the music. And the best way to express ourselves is through music. When you stand up there, it (music) releases the tension, no matter what your situation is. It's as if you have become something else. And the joy of fulfilling people's hopes and bringing joy to them! There is nothing that can describe this feeling."

She has not forgotten the people who shaped her as a musician. "In the early days my father was my influence. When I came to Johannesburg there were other musicians – people like Duke Makasi, Abigail Kubeka and Sammy Brown, who had faith in me," says Felicia, who spent many hungry days at Dorkay House, honing her skills.

She adds: "There were also people like Miriam Makeba and Hugh Masekela, with whom I worked between 1988 and 1990, travelling worldwide. They taught me the tricks of the game."

Has she any advice for aspirant musicians?

Felicia answers that there is indeed a lot she can say. "When I started the whole thing, I was a quiet person, very introverted. Until I got caught up in the swing of things. Unfortunately I did many things which I now regret.

"For some reason, when you are in music, you believe that you have to live a certain life. It's not true. But when you are young and have the world at your feet and you have hits, you don't think soberly. You are immature.

"I dabbled in many things, such as light drugs, and I used to drink a lot. I don't know why. I wouldn't say it was for a specific reason. But I felt there was an emptiness somewhere. I would be so happy, out there performing, but as soon as I got home I would be lonely. You know, inside me. Even if I was with people, I felt that nobody understood and appreciated me.

"Young people must understand that music is a gift, and it needs to be properly nurtured. You should also take care of your personal life, which should not fall apart just because you are in music."

Interviewed at her home in Johannesburg in 1993

Gusta Mnguni

To this day, Gusta Mnguni believes that her performance in the South African musical *Phiri* was the zenith of her career as a singer.

Hundreds of show-goers who packed Soweto's Diepkloof Hall sat transfixed and awe-struck at her polished singing in the star-studded show – particularly when she put her heart and soul into the poignant song "Whose Earth is This?". Many likened Gusta's gutsy and spirited performance to the American superstar entertainer Barbra Streisand.

Looking back to that 1972 première of the show, Gusta smiles and explains: "Maybe the reason why our people loved the show was that in those days white authority perceived it as nothing but 'black subversive' politics. The show had a strong message. It was a show that also made me strong as a singer."

Gusta, like scores of African women singers, started out in a church choir. Her father made sure that she never absconded from the choir rehearsals in their Radium Mission village in Warmbaths in the former Eastern Transvaal.

"When I joined our school choir, I went straight to the seniors. I was the youngest member of the choir. Come to think of it, I was a mere eight years old."

While she was at high school, her father wanted her to learn dressmaking. She enrolled for a six-month course at a boarding school in Evaton, south of Johannesburg in the Vereeniging district.

"After finishing the dressmaking course I decided to look for a job in a clothing factory, even though I nursed an ambition to become a singer. Not many people, including my parents and relatives, were aware of my secret ambition," she recalls.

Fortune smiled on Gusta. A woman she had met, one of the few people who knew of her ambition to become a singer, knew the agent Hugo Keleti, who had singers like Tandie Klaasen and Busi (Viccie) Mhlongo on his books.

Kelleti offered Gusta a job as a secretary. Her main functions were "to take messages in the office. And collect monthly fees from the students he was tutoring in music. He also taught me basic book-keeping.".

The desire to become a singer saw Gusta joining a male street busker on the busy streets of Hillbrow, at the time home to numerous bohemians.

"And I was starting to make money," laughs Gusta. At that time she was interested in all things musical. She frequently visited the famous Bantu Men's Social Centre – "where I used to enjoy watching people dance".

It was during one of these visits to the Centre that she met Sam Williams, leader of the singing group the Wavers. By then Gusta and her group of buskers used to rehearse at the now-demolished Harlem Cinema, not far from the Centre.

Williams insisted that she had a good voice and should join a music company. He suggested she join composer-playwright Gibson Kente.

"That is how I joined Kente's *Lifa*, which featured top-liners Mabel Mafuya, Patric Ndlovu, Viccie Mhlongo and Zakes Khuse. My second musical with Kente was *Zwi*, before joining Williams in *The Question*. It was after this box-office disaster that I heard of the *Phiri* auditions. I went and Davashe took me on the spot."

After that Gusta had a brief fling with what could have been her passport to fame and fortune. She joined the musical *Ipi Tombi*, whose Johannesburg première in 1974 was followed by performance in London and a tour to Australia. She never made the overseas tour.

"I was fired from the show after two months." Gusta's openness about "the misundertanding with the management" of the show is almost childlike.

Then she found work with the rock musical *Hair* – at the time banned in South Africa – and had to join the cast in neighbouring Lesotho. There were brief immigration problems which forced her to return to South Africa. When she had sorted out the immigration problems and rejoined the show, she "found that things didn't work out well (for her) and had to come back home to South Africa."

Steady work came her way in 1975 when she joined Abigail Kubeka in a show in one of Johannesburg's top clubs, The Pit. She later joined Taubie Kushlick's production of *Porgy and Bess* at the city's famous Alhambra Theatre in Doornfontein.

Things were going well for Gusta when she joined jazz pianist Pat Matshikiza in cabaret at a well-known city night club. But her partnership with Matshikiza was short-lived, as the theatre bar in the then famous Brooke Theatre in the city, where they doubled up on their cabaret circuit, was closed down by the police in 1980.

Gusta went into semi-retirement, performing infrequently. In 1990, she was teaching voice training and singing to children at a inner-city Johannesburg college.

Why didn't she go overseas when she was at the peak of her career? It is a painful answer that she gives, but it centres around her love for her father. "When I was on tour, I would send him money but he said he didn't need it. He wanted me to be around him because one day he would die. He died in 1989."

Gusta – whose major influences were voice trainer Ann Fielder and American greats Sarah Vaughan and Nina Simone – predicts a bright future for African women singers.

"Yes, there was segregation when we started out in our careers. But now that's a thing of the past. That's why I want to start or be attached to a music school. So that I'm remembered and leave something behind for my people. I want that to be my monument."

Interviewed at a Johannesburg club, 1993

Isabella Masote

Like most African women singers, Isabella's career started in church. To be precise, at the Anglican Church of St Bernard The Martyr in Atteridgeville outside Pretoria.

It was in that church choir that she first had the taste of classical works – Handel's *Messiah*, for instance – under well-known conductor and community leader Michael Rantho.

It was an accomplished choir, and it was no surprise when PACT (Performing Arts Council of the Transvaal) invited its members to sing in the chorus of one of its concerts.

"We sang the Slave Chorus from the opera *Aida*. It was from there that I developed an interest in and love for classic music," laughs Isabella, emphasising the word "slave".

There was another concert at Pretoria's St Alban's Cathedral, which was to launch her into her classical music career. Professor Rudolf van Alk, who taught music at the Pretoria Technikon, happened to be in the audience. He was greatly impressed by her singing, and after the concert he approached her and suggested that she get classical music training.

"But I did not know where to go for training. Later I made an application to the well-known South African classical opera singer Mimi Coertze, the Vienna-trained singer who returned to South Africa after working for the Vienna State Opera for many years. She was known to encourage and foster talent by advising young singers. This was round about 1980/81.

"She suggested that I contact the Pretoria Technikon," Isabella recalls.

In turn the Pretoria Technikon invited Isabella for an audition. At the audition she sang a solo from Handel's *Messiah*. The Technikon teachers were impressed.

"They were interested in my voice, but realised that I had no money for tuition." One of the teachers, Eric Muller, offered her private guidance and tuition for free. Then a woman who was working for the United States Embassy in Pretoria chipped in and offered to pay Isabella's fees at the Technikon. This opened further doors for Isabella, who was later granted an Ernest Oppenheimer scholarship by the Anglo-American Corporation.

"In addition to the Oppenheimer Scholarship, I received a R10 000 scholarship from the German car manufacturer BMW, because people realised that there was promise in my voice," Isabella says with the confidence of a young woman who knows where she is heading and what she wants.

In 1988, after three years of hard work and study, Isabella found herself to be one of the students employed by PACT.

During her studies, she proudly reminds you, she sang the part of the Countess in Mozart's *Le Nozze di Figaro* and Constance in Poulens' *Dialogues des Carmelites* at the Roodepoort City Theatre. In 1988 PACT employed her full-time as a junior soloist. But the ambitious Isabella felt isolated; she was hungry for experience and work in the concert hall. She explains: "To sing full-time, as a junior soloist, didn't give me the chance and I didn't like it."

When interviewed, she was full-time with the PACT chorus. (Since the beginning of 1997, when PACT underwent restructuring she has been a freelance singer.) It was a hard, demanding job. Her typical day consisted of two sessions of two hours each, with another session in the evening.

"All this means that I appear in every opera production. We have just finished *Rigoletto*. We are busy with *Madama Butterfly* at the Pretoria State Opera." Isabella confesses that her dream is to sing at the world's great opera houses – Milan's La Scala, London's Covent Garden and The Metropolitan in New York City.

In 1992 she performed as a soloist in PACT's production of *Death in Venice*. She has also appeared as an oratorio soloist in concert halls in Johannesburg and Pretoria, as well as in soirees and television productions.

Isabella believes that classical music is gaining popular support. She bases her belief on previous work she has done with the PACT Orchestra when they toured the black townships. "The reaction and acceptance was fantastic," she says. "We are making progress. I receive a lot of phone calls from children who want to be trained and educated in classical music. I have to be patient with the young ones when I explain that in this career you can't start when you are too young, you have to start in your early twenties."

She is amused by the question whether classical music will catch the imagination of Africans, and if there is any risk of it being labelled an elitist "white" cultural form.

"Africans are already into classical music in a big way," she replies. She points out that choral music has made a resurgence in African communities since the 1980s. This, she argues, is a strong pointer that classical music has already taken strong root. The well-patronised and acclaimed annual Sowetan/Caltex Massed Choirs Festival illustrates this trend.

"Choral music is classical music. There are also the story-telling aspects of the opera which will connect with my people's culture. You know, the fireside tales."

Isabella Masote's voice is no doubt one of the instruments that will bring the joy of classical music to even more people!

Interviewed at her home in Atteridgeville outside Pretoria in 1993

Letta Mbulu

American music superstar Quincy Jones described Letta Mbulu's music as something that expresses hope, joy and determination, and an unconquerable spirit. "It expresses hope for the future because we know it belongs to us," he said in 1975 while working with her on the soundtrack of the mini-series *Roots*.

Today Mbulu has reached the top as an accomplished international artist. She has graced the stages of the world, where her incredible vocal range and control have brought audiences to their feet. Her approach to music is very African yet manages to be international and sophisticated at the same time. The fact that all the albums she released in South Africa have achieved platinum status (50 000 units) is proof of her success.

Praise was also heaped on her in the United States, where she spent 26 years. Millions of viewers heard her sing the theme song of the blockbuster television mini-series *Roots*. For her performance in that production Letta received an Emmy, as well a gold disc for 500 000 record sales within the first month of the soundtrack's release.

She has done more recording in the United States. Her voice can be heard in Michael Jackson's song "Liberian Girl" on his *Bad* album, and she was the narrator in *You Struck a Rock*, a documentary film that examined the role of women in South Africa's political struggle.

Other screen credits include working with American legend Sidney Poitier in *Warm December* and with Steven Spielberg in *The Colour Purple*.

It has been a steady climb for Letta since her first major engagement in the United States in the sixties: a performance at the Village Gate in New York City which won her critical acclaim. When she was subsequently invited to tour with the late Julian "Cannonball" Adderley, her feet were firmly on the ladder to success.

But Letta returned to South Africa in 1990. Today she sees a bigger role and responsibility for her and fellow African artists who have made it big overseas.

"I have to plough back what they, my community, gave me as a young woman. Young people need to be shown what to do, told of the importance of being an artist. The importance of being a performer is not glamour but hard work."

Letta continues: "I have a responsibility. The community looks at you and you become your community. These are some of the things we have to impart to our young people."

As founder member of South African Artists United, which was launched in the USA in 1986, she is working hard at fulfilling that responsibility. The organisation's first offering was *Buwa*, which toured throughout Africa from early 1987 until November 1988 and in which she played a leading role.

But where did this impressive career start? Letta thinks back to the dusty streets of Orlando East, Soweto. In 1956 Jimmy Mabena, a musician who had a knack to spot talent, heard her sing and introduced her to an up-and-coming close-harmony group, the Swanky Spots. The ball started rolling.

"In fact, the Swanky Spots are the ones that made me understand that I wanted to be a singer. All of us in the group were the same age, disciplined and wanting to be in the music business. We wanted to sing."

Letta and the Swanky Spots caught the attention of many a music lover when they walked away with the first prize in a talent contest organised by Union Artists in 1957. The young group had a firm foot in the door.

The strong community support Letta and the Swanky Spots enjoyed was invaluable to the young singer. "The people understood where I came from, and I understood where they came from. This is the community that wanted to see something good come out of Soweto, out of Orlando East. They encouraged us because they saw a spark of light in us."

From singing in a close-harmony group, Letta moved on into a musical environment which exposed her to influences far beyond her traditional folk music and the sounds of urban South Africa.

Like most of her contemporaries, she had to undergo the baptism of fire in the revue *African Jazz and Variety*, which was winning kudo after kudo on its tours of South Africa and neighbouring countries.

Then in 1959, still only thirteen years old, she won a part in *King Kong*. After an extended tour through South Africa and a year-long run in the United Kingdom, Letta was among those artists who returned to South Africa.

But a polished and fiercely ambitious Letta, who desperately wanted to succeed, found the South African climate of the sixties stifling to her artistic development and freedom. The apartheid policies of the time finally forced her to leave in 1961 and seek greener pastures overseas.

Ask her about her musical inspiration, the men and women who challenged her to be the best, and she rattles off names that sound like a Who's Who of urban South African show business of the fifties: Dolly Rathebe, Dorothy Masuka, the Manhattan Brothers, the Woody Woodpeckers, the Dark City Sisters, Ben "Satch" Masinga, Mackay Davashe.

"And, of course, there were people I have never met. But their music stayed with me. Like Alan Silinga, who composed the evergreen 'Ntyilo Ntyilo'. There was also Nomonde Sihawu from Benoni and Mabel Magada from Port Elizabeth. I had my role models, fantastic musicians. There was so much to draw on."

There was also Letta's family connection which contributed to her musical development: her mother Elda, who died in 1978, was an accomplished singer.

"There was always music in our house. And I couldn't resist it." Saying that, Letta Mbulu's face breaks into that warm smile which has captivated millions of music lovers from so many album covers.

Interviewed in the Yard of Ale Restaurant, Johannesburg, 1993

Lynette Leeuw

Desperation launched Lynette Leeuw's career: her recording studio was desperate for a hit. It was 1962 and in a bid to hit the big time, the Riviera Recording Studio in Doornfontein, Johannesburg, came up with the idea of recording a woman playing saxophone.

After all, in the early sixties mbaqanga was the big-selling sound in both the urban and rural music market in South Africa. It was unheard of to have a female instrumentalist doing mbaqanga – traditionally the female artists did only vocals, while the men played the instruments (as well as did vocals). Lynette's studio wanted something different.

"In fact," laughs Lynette, "the studio wanted a marketing gimmick. They desperately needed a hit. They took me and showed me how to play an alto saxophone. They made me practice the instrument for two hours, and the following day a studio was booked for a recording."

It is now history that Lynette's debut as a saxophonist – *Girls Can Blow, Volume 1* – became a hit and launched her on an amazing music career.

She tells what happened after the record was made: "I recorded with a multi-racial studio band and virtually hours after the record had hit the stores, we received reports from the sales people that it had sold more than 11 000 copies. We had an instant hit.

"I had to record follow-up records for *Girls Can Blow*, a series which went up to volume four. But I did it with a different studio, Teal Records, because my original studio folded. So they said, but I think they had made a lot of money and had no reason to continue."

Lynette's career took a dramatic turn when she worked for Teal. She had to tour the areas where her records were sold "because most of the people couldn't believe that a woman could play the saxophone.

"I became what was known in the trade as a 'personal advert'. We toured country-wide, even Lesotho and Swaziland, playing in record shops. People had to see me playing the saxophone. Even in the

halls where I was performing, they came in their numbers because most thought I was a man dressed in a woman's clothing."

But Lynette was hungry and ambitious to master her alto saxophone. Maybe the musicians she admired had something to do with it. They included Zakes Nkosi, Victor Ndlazilwane and the American jazzman Johnny Hodges.

"I wanted to play well and improve. At first I tried to teach myself to master the instrument, but it did not work out. Then I enrolled at the FUBA (Federated Union of Black Artists) Academy in Johannesburg where I took music theory lessons in 1987. But before that, Ndlazilwana was a great help and inspiration when he took me through the basics of the instrument, teaching and showing me things like scales."

Today Lynette is competent in reading and writing music. But it took a lot of effort to get where she is. Her only advantage when she decided to become a musician was that she came from a musical family. Her father was a well-known West Rand church choir conductor and her mother an able musician.

"I think I took after my parents. When I was growing up we even had a family choir in our house – my father, mother and my sisters and I sang and entertained ourselves and relatives. Later it became easier when we formed the Leeuw Sisters," Lynette says of her formative years in Madubulaville, outside Randfontein.

Her ability and talent to sing was also an advantage at school. She was a popular singer who always took the lead parts at school concerts and had no problem with her Catholic nun teachers "when they taught us Latin church hymns."

Lynette entered show business when she formed the Randfontein Dolls in 1961. It was a short-lived group which first recorded hymns and then graduated to mbaqanga. At the same time, she was gaining experience and writing her own songs.

"So when I started the Leeuw Sisters in 1970 everything fell into place because they knew how to sing and I had a good idea of the music industry," laughs Lynette, who has worked and rubbed shoulders with popular singers like Mary Thobei, Dorothy Masuka, Kori Morara and later, in the eighties, Hugh Masekela in Botswana.

Lynette can't remember how many records she has made. Part of the problem is that for many years South African recording studios used African singers in many and various formats and under different labels.

"That is why I'd sometimes be travelling in a taxi and hear a song with a familiar melody being played. Then after some time, something would click in my memory and I would realise that it was my song, maybe recorded years ago," she says.

Lynette was influenced by the American gospel singer Mahalia Jackson, jazzman Johnny Hodges and South Africans Ntemi Piliso and Zakes Nkosi. But she has always admired male musicians who played instruments because "there were no women instrumentalists among our people and I wanted to play like those men."

Music – any good and meaningful music – always touches her in one way or the other. She can be moved to tears by songs she hears on the radio, TV or performed live by other artists.

Sometimes the music she plays is inspired by her audiences. If ever her playing is flat or uninspired she immediately feels it, because that moment – whether it is at a live performance or in a studio – becomes musically meaningless.

For Lynette Leeuw, there can be nothing worse.

(Sadly, Lynette Leeu died suddenly on 31 July 1997 while on a fund-raising tour in Swaziland.)

Interviewed at Dorkay House, Johannesburg, in 1993

Mabel Mafuya

Mabel Mafuya tells a story which illustrates her desire to become a singer as a little girl growing up in Soweto in the early fifties.

One afternoon she and a few friends saw Dolly Rathebe walking down a street in Orlando East. When the great "Queen of the Blues" passed the group of admiring girls, she happened to throw away the apple she was eating.

"I rushed and picked up the half-eaten apple and took a good bite," Mabel laughs as she recalls the incident. "My mind and heart told me that if I bit that apple where the great Dolly had bitten, I would grow up and sing like her one day."

But Mabel was already stage-struck, even before she met Dolly on the street in Orlando East. She was particularly impressed by the music of another great singer of the era, Dorothy Masuka.

"When I heard Dorothy sing her hit song 'Notsokolo' on the radio and on records, I loved her. We idolised singers like Dorothy and Dolly."

Little did Mabel dream that she would one day team up with Dorothy and Dolly. This opportunity came when Mabel joined the top recording studio of the time, Troubadour.

"This was after the late Cuthbert Madumba, the talent scout for Troubadour, discovered me while I was still a student at Orlando High School. When I started I didn't know much about singing. But Dorothy showed me the ropes." Mabel does not hide her appreciation for the help she received in those early years.

Her career blossomed when she came out with the hits "Hula Hoop" and "Nomathemba", which caught the imagination of the black townships. She led the group the Green Lanterns and soon became one of the most prolific vocalists of the mid- to late-fifties, recording with a number of top singers, among others Mary Thobei and Caroline Maluleke.

Shortly afterwards, Mabel, Mary Thobei and Thandeka Mpambane formed the Chord Sisters, a teenage group modelled on the high-riding Quad Sisters. The era which was dominated by another all-female group, the Skylarks.

Mabel gives a throaty laugh when she remembers that her Orlando East "home-girl" Letta Mbulu was still very young then. "Those were the days. We loved it. We used to record twice or thrice a week. There was also stage work, which we loved. I think what we did was essentially driven by our love for music.

"But," Mabel's features darken, "there was music on the one hand and exploitation on the other. Fortunately, we trampled on the exploitation and our frustration with our songs."

Mabel's career was badly affected when a goitre operation went wrong in 1957. Thereafter her musical career "began an inexorable downhill decline". However, around 1959 her career took a turn for the better. She got a small part in the jazz-opera *King Kong*, the cast of which included most prominent figures of African song and dance of the time.

"I remember Miriam (Makeba) pleading and pleading with me to take part in the musical. I did my small part, though I did not know what acting was all about. But Leon Gluckman, the director, told me I could act. He took me to drama teacher Nora Taylor for acting lessons." Mabel shakes her head in amazement.

King Kong was to be Mabel's life, as the jazz-opera performed before sold-out audiences on a South African nationwide tour. Gluckman's confidence in her as an actress was finally vindicated when *King Kong* went to England in 1961 and he took her to a London drama school.

Mabel remembers the year in London as a period of being schooled in the intricacies of acting. When *King Kong* ended its tour in 1962, she was among those artists who returned to South Africa rather than pursue their careers overseas.

"I was unfortunate that the plays which appealed to me in South Africa, and in which I performed later, were political works," she says without emotion.

Some of the plays were in fact banned for what the authorities perceived to be highly political content. They included *Confused Mhlaba*, *A Matter of Convenience* and *The Talking Ghost* in 1988, her last play.

"There is nothing I loved more than acting. After my stint with *King Kong* I still loved acting, as long as the works spoke the truth," says Mabel, who later also starred in one of South Africa's best-loved African television situation comedies, *Velaphi*, in which she played the role of Nombi.

But there were harrowing moments in her career as a musician that Mabel cannot forget. She was assaulted after she and Mary Thobei recorded the hit "King Kong Oshwile, Ma", which lionised legendary boxer Ezekiel "King Kong" Dlamini. Dlamini tragically died at a prison farm after being sentenced for murder.

According to Mabel, when the record hit the market, there was a misconception from Dlamini's colleagues, friends and family that the song was mocking King Kong. "One day his friends from the Jeppe Men's Hostel caught up with me at the Jeppe railway station. I woke up in the Johannesburg General Hospital, badly beaten up."

Being a female and a singer also held other risks for Mabel and most of her contemporaries. She tells story after story of the tsotsi terror at halls.

But for Mabel the fifties were beautiful times – what Joseph Mogotsi of the Manhattan Brothers describes as "jazzy times". Of course, she says, her parents were against a singer's career for her at first but they finally relented when they discovered how determined she was.

Mabel laments the missing continuity of a solid music tradition in South Africa. According to her, the young singers nowadays seem to have no idea of where they come from.

"They don't know us. But I don't blame them. Nobody told them about us."

Interviewed at home in Orlando East in 1993

Mabel Magada

Many jazz lovers of the fifties and sixties still swear that no one could sing the blues like Mabel Magada. From film to drama to live reviews, Mabel built a reputation as one of the finest vocalists of her generation.

Where did this successful career start? Mabel was born in Graaff-Reinet. After school she enrolled as a student nurse at Baragwanath Hospital in Soweto. But fate had other plans. Her mother got ill, and before the completion of her studies, Mabel moved back to the Eastern Cape to be with her mother in Port Elizabeth. By that time, however, Mabel had discovered that she could sing, and she joined a local band, the King Cole Basies, and became their vocalist.

She was visiting an aunt in Germiston in 1953 when a friend told her about auditions for a film. After much persuasion she took up the challenge and presented herself for the audition at the Bantu Men's Social Centre, at that stage the hub of social activity for Africans on the Reef.

"I found the big names in show business at the audition. There were stars like Dolly Rathebe and Ribbon Dlamini. I felt I would not make it, but all the same when my turn came I sang. Imagine my surprise when I learnt that I had won the leading role!"

The film, *The Song of Africa*, took about six months to finish and featured, among others, the African Inkspots. After filming, Mabel once again returned to Port Elizabeth. She plunged into work with a number of musicians and formed the Keynotes, a vocal group which included Norman Ntshinga, who was to become Mabel's husband in 1959.

The Keynotes soon disbanded, but she did not let up on her stage work. She branched out into drama, joining the Serpent Players – who, in years to come, would win popularity countrywide and internationally with works by John Kani, Winston Ntshona and Athol Fugard. While working with the Serpent Players, Mabel won praise as the governor's wife

in Fugard's adaption of Berthold Brecht's *The Caucasian Chalk Circle*.

Then the late Ian Bernhardt, a prominent impresario, wanted her in Johannesburg for *Beyond the Blues*, a trailblazing show combining jazz and poetry, which was to run at the Wits University Great Hall in Johannesburg in 1963. With this show Mabel, in the company of actor Zakes Mokae, who read highly charged poetry by leading African-American poets, and Chris McGregor's Blue Notes, introduced a new dimension to South African music in general and jazz in particular.

Jazz fans were eating out of Mabel's hand. Shortly after *Beyond the Blues* she was in another scorcher of a show – *Swinging the Blues*, with musical arrangements by Chris McGregor. Mabel and her group, the Maytones – with singers Nomonde Sihawu, Vinah Bendile and Zelda Malgas – gave a sparkling performance that made them the toast of the town overnight. After this triumph, Mabel returned to Port Elizabeth once again.

When asked about her inspiration as a jazz singer, Mabel rattles off names like Ella Fitzgerald, Sarah Vaughan and Gloria Lynn. And, of course, Emily Kwenane. "I loved her, she was a powerhouse." Other influences include Dolly Rathebe, Sophie Mgcina and Letta Mbulu.

But, according to Mabel, the biggest dues go to her cousin, Seun ("Boy" in English) Vena, who grew up with her at her grandmother's house in Graaff-Reinet and attended the famous Eastern Cape Healdtown School: "He taught us to sing

jazz. And when I heard his records of people like Ella and Sarah Vaughan, I immediately loved them."

Mabel laughs heartily when she recalls her cousin's old-fashioned gramophone, which made it all happen for her.

"That's how I fell in love with jazz. Since then I was never able to get out of it, up to this day. Have you seen my jazz record collection?" Mabel opens a room in her house and the stacks of records she displays prove her point beyond doubt.

There is vigour in her voice when she talks about what she considers to have been the highlight of her career. In a voice a few decibels higher with excitement, she states without hesitation: the *Beyond the Blues* show at Wits University was the big one. "I still have newspaper clippings of that show."

But she has won a greater prize. In 1992 the Port Elizabeth community organised a mammoth celebration in her honour. A handsome trophy, which occupies a place of pride on her mantelpiece, is a souvenir of that community gesture. It is simply inscribed: "To Mabel Magada, in recognition of your contribution to music and the dramatic arts."

For Mabel, this is the greatest accolade of them all: "It was the first time I discovered that Port Elizabeth's people loved me. I broke down when they asked me at the function to give a speech. There was a lump in my throat. I did not expect it. I felt like a queen that night.'

But life has also dealt her some disappointments. She still wonders what course her career would have taken if she had taken the leading female role in *King Kong* in 1959.

"Leon Gluckman, the producer, had secured the part for me. I had to get on a train to Johannesburg on a Sunday and start rehearsals on Tuesday with the rest of the cast. Unfortunately urgent family matters prevented this. It just didn't work out."

Interviewed at her home in KwaMagxaki outside Port Elizabeth, 1993

Mahotella Queens

When the high-riding Mahotella Queens left on 14 February 1993 – St Valentine's Day – for a six-month tour to Japan, Australia, New Zealand, Europe and the United States, they believed it was a good omen.

"This time it shows we are going to spread love worldwide through our music. We are leaving on a day when everybody spreads love around," laughed Hilda Tloubatla, Nobesuthu Shawe and Mildred Mangxola when interviewed shortly before.

The trio pointed out that since 1987, when they hit the international market with a sell-out tour of France, it had almost become a ritual that they would leave South Africa every year in January or February for an overseas tour.

"When we come back home after an overseas tour, we find that we have already been booked for the same time the following year. That has been our schedule since 1987," said Hilda.

The Mahotella Queens started out as a five-women group. In those early days, when their mqashiyo and simanje-manje brand of music emerged in the African townships of South Africa, they were the three current members plus Juliet Mazamisa and Ethel Mngomezulu. They had no formal training.

Somehow, record producer Rupert Bopape was responsible for the Mahotella/Mahlathini magic. In 1961, when he joined Gallo, he hit on the idea of Simon "Mahlathini" Nkabinde, the king of South African groaners, and the Mahotella Queens. After all, it was fashionable for every simanje-manje group to feature a male "groaner" in its line-up and repertoire.

Their innovative dance routines based on traditional steps and urban jive helped to make the new combined musical force an instant hit.

With the passing of time Juliet and Ethel dropped out and the Queens gradually disappeared from the South African music scene. In 1983 Hilda, Nobesuthu and Mildred got together again and revived the group. They had met well-known record producer West Nkosi, who invited them to give performances in France.

Nobesuthu remembers: "That French show was a hit. Before that sell-out French tour we were a little afraid of the reception. But Nkosi assured us that the French loved us already because they had been listening to our records."

It was a small but significant beginning for the Queens. Then came 1988, when they appeared with Mahlathini at the Nelson Mandela Birthday Concert at London's giant Wembley Stadium before thousands of excited music fans as well as millions of television viewers worldwide.

That Wembley concert started a ripple effect that saw numerous invitations arrive at their Johannesburg office, with offers of lucrative tours to numerous countries around the world.

The Queens were the only South African group to be invited to sing at the 1992 Olympic Games in Barcelona, and also to play at the prestigious Club Quattro in Tokyo, Japan.

What is the secret of the Queens' success? Hilda, Nobesuthu and Mildred agree: "People just love our Zulu music. In truth, we work very hard at it. We do everything on our own. Choreography, compositions and almost everything that must be done.

"Maybe, on the other hand, it is our belief that if the Queens would take another musical direction, it would be our downfall. We would fall out of favour with our fans. They want us as we are, with our music and traditional costumes. We are also sure that if anybody would try to imitate us and go for our market, he or she would find that audiences want the Mahotella Queens and nothing else."

That is the down-to-earth philosophy of the Queens, with their backing band Makhona Tsohle and fourth voice, Simon "Mahlathini" Nkabinde.

Nobesuthu adds: "Take Japan, for instance. The way they love our music is unbelievable." In appreciation for the enthusiastic support they had in Japan, the Queens decided to record an album of a capella songs especially for their fans in Japan.

Hilda, Nobesuthu and Midred feel that have not been influenced by anybody in their music and careers but believe they are gifted singers blessed with old-fashioned talent, capacity for hard work and a knack of doing the right thing at the right time.

But they also believe that their compositions, which tell of their experiences as ordinary Africans in South Africa, have something to do with their appeal. And this also explains why they have stuck with Zulu lyrics, which according to them work better to express the message they want to get across to their audiences.

"There are people who can handle English lyrics better than we can. There are musicians like Lionel Ritchie, who do a better job in that department. Also very important is that our fans love us singing in our native language. Singing in that language has become our trademark," Hilda argues.

In all, the Queens say they are humbled to know that they are doing something positive with their music. They are particularly grateful for the workshops they are able to hold when they are on tour in the United States, where they teach children the songs, traditions and culture of Africans in South Africa.

Another contribution of which the Queens are proud is the message of the strength of women worldwide that are expressed on their 1990 album, *Women of the World*.

The Mahotella Queens, who have shared a stage with some of the top musicians in the world, including Sonny Rollins, the late Sonny Stitt, Ray Charles, Jimmy Cliff and the Commodores, are not yet thinking of retirement.

"The older you get, the more you improve in this business," says Hilda.

Ask them about the future and the Queens answer almost in unison: "We ask God to bless us and help us to continue singing. Through our music we managed to feed and clothe our families."

What about the future? "We ask God to bless us and our work."

Mildred Mangxolo, Nobesuthu Shawe and Hilda Tloubatla interviewed at Downtown Studios, Johannesburg, January 1993

Mandisa Gwele-Maepa

Strike action at the University of Fort Hare in 1971 might have put paid to the dreams of Mandisa Gwele-Maepa's parents of her becoming a medical doctor, but for Mandisa it meant a whole new life in show business.

She was studying for a Bachelor of Science degree which would have been the stepping stone towards medical studies.

"It is interesting. It was not my intention to be in show business professionally," Mandisa explains. "My parents wanted me to be a medical doctor, simply because I was good at mathematics and science. So my career was decided for me."

But when strike action broke out, Mandisa left university. She was in limbo. At that time her parents lived in Dayeyton, Benoni. One of the hottest bands in the township – in fact, in the whole province – was the Jazz Ministers, under the able leadership of Victor Ndlazilwana.

"I decided to join them just to while away time. I initiated the process when I approached their trumpeter, Johnny Mekoa."

An impromptu audition was arranged at Mandisa's home, where there was a piano. At the audition, Mekoa was at the piano and Mandisa had to sing.

"I don't remember what I sang," she continues, "but I think it was one of Ella Fitzgerald's songs that was popular at the time. At the end of it, Mekoa was smiling and nodding his head. And I was in. From then on I began to be known as a jazz singer."

Two years later, in 1973, Mandisa joined the cast of the cabaret show *Meropa*, which was destined for a Far East tour. The show had been put together by impresario Clarence Wilson. Auditions where held at Dorkay House, Johannesburg's beehive of black song, dance and drama. The novelty of overseas travel drove Mandisa, who had never done traditional music and dance before, to go for an audition.

Later that year, after a number of shows in Johannesburg, Cape Town and Durban, *Meropa* left for Japan, Hong Kong and the Philippines. After a successful run in the Far East, the show was back in South Africa with firm commitments that it

would make annual return visits to the Far East. But politics came into the picture and changed everything.

"Japan broke all diplomatic ties with South Africa. In any case, it appeared at the time that Clarence didn't have definite plans for the show. So when the return-visit to Japan fell through, impresario Louis Burke and his wife Joan Brickhill took an interest in the show.

"Burke and Brickhill turned the show into a big theatrical production, expanded the cast from twelve to 32 and introduced a story line. There was also a name change: from *Meropa* to *KwaZulu*. In 1975 the show went to London.

"We spent three months at the New London Theatre, then moved to the Piccadilly Theatre in the West End, where we spent eight months. All in all, we spent almost a year in London."

Somehow this long absence from home and her country suited Mandisa well. After all, hers had always been a family constantly on the move.

She continues: "When I was growing up at my grandparents' home in Roodepoort, my family moved to Brakpan, Benoni, Bloemfontein, Grahamstown, Kokstad, Umtata . The only province my family never lived in when South Africa had four provinces was Natal.

"You see, my dad had a very adventurous streak. And I have inherited that. We would go on holiday to a place and Dad would like it. In no time, the family would move there. At the same time he would promise to take us someplace else. We would be excited, but he would abruptly change his mind and we would move somewhere else entirely. And there would be no explanation from him for that sudden change of mind."

So Mandisa was well used to travel. For her the highlight of her singing career

was the Royal Command Performance of *KwaZulu* for Britain's Queen Elizabeth II.

"A Royal Command Performance is real special. There's no question about it. And in the cast of 32 were Mara Louw, Victor Ntoni, Thapelo Mofokeng and a host of other talented performers, most of whom are big in show business today."

Unfortunately when the *KwaZulu* cast came back home to South Africa, the anti-apartheid political climate was red-hot. There was the pressure of a cultural boycott and sanctions from abroad, and *KwaZulu* did not survive; it could not undertake further overseas tours.

Mandisa then entered the cabaret circuit, doing shows countrywide and also at hotel venues in Lesotho, Swaziland and the former Transkei. She warmly remembers a gig she did in Umtata in the seventies with the now internationally acclaimed jazz pianist, saxophonist and composer, Bheki Mseleku.

When Mandisa says Mseleku is "a brilliant pianist", she does not make that judgement casually. She comes from a family of pianists – her father was a solid pianist who joined her mother in roaring music sessions at their home; her uncle, the late Boysie Gwele, was considered one of the South African jazz greats in the forties.

Mandisa's main influences were American singers Sarah Vaughan, Ella Fitzgerald and Nancy Wilson. (In fact, Mandisa's middle name is Nancy, named after the singer by her grandmother.)

Towards the end of the seventies Mandisa's exciting but brief career came to a close. "It was no longer a paying proposition, so I decided to retire from show business," she explains.

Today Mandisa is a prominent figure in corporate South Africa. She serves on the board of directors of nine companies and organisations. This shift started in 1987 when she was the first black woman to be appointed a manager by the Standard Bank Group. Since then she has done a variety of high-powered jobs as she mapped out a challenging new route for herself.

Interviewed at her Bedfordview home, Johannesburg, in 1993

Mara Louw

What more could any South African artist want than an audience of 600 million television viewers in 60 countries worldwide?

Add to this some of the most glamorous actors and actresses, socialites and supermodels, as well as musicians like Yvonne Chaka Chaka, Abigail Kubeka, MarcAlex and the Soweto String Quartet sharing the stage. And, of course, the sheer size and magic of the occasion itself – the 1992 Miss World beauty pageant at Sun City.

But Mara Louw, one of the pageant's shining stars, doesn't dwell overly much on that evening. Not that this singer, who started her career at the age of eleven singing in a Soweto choral group, regards the Miss World appearance as meaningless. It's just that Mara is a perfectionist who is always looking forward and refuses to dwell on past glory and achievement. "You are as good as your last show," she says succinctly.

She continues: "I am still trying to get to the top, working very hard to improve my career. In South Africa you can't get to the stage where you can say you've done it all. Every day you learn, new things are happening. Every day I'm learning. I'll eventually get there when the time is ripe. I am not going to say I know it all just because I have been in the business for 23 years."

And it has been an eventful 23 years. After returning to South Africa in 1976 from an overseas tour with the musical *Meropa*, she worked as a solo artist. In 1984 her star shone brightly when she won both Radio Sotho and Radio Zulu's Best Female Vocalist award, and was nominated for the SABC's premier award, the Artes.

Beyond her native land's borders, Mara has performed for some of the great leaders on the African continent. She sang at a private function for former Zambian president Kenneth Kaunda in Lusaka, and also for Zimbabwe's president Robert Mugabe and his vice-president Joshua Nkomo at a conferene at Victoria Falls.

Mara says that many things have kept her going as an artist. These include the political situation in South Africa, and also an unshakable belief that she had to

prove to herself, her family and friends that she could do it and that she would not let them down.

"Politically speaking, I did it because as an oppressed person in South Africa, I felt it my duty to do the best in my career and prove to the white man that I could do it. We (Africans) have been undermined, we have been given a rotten education which was meant to keep us maids or garden boys.

"So to show that someone can do something if they are given the chance, I got into different avenues of show business. Firstly to prove a point, and secondly because I loved doing it."

Mara has come a long way since her teens, when she sang for one of Soweto's best-known choral groups, the Wilba Music Group, under Wilby Baqwa. But even then, everybody was soon commenting on the quality of her voice.

With the late Wilby Baqwa Mara took her first steps on the road to a singing career. Her late sister did her part by introducing her to the music of the great gospel singer Mahalia Jackson. The young singer also spent a lot of time listening to Duke Ellington and Ella Fitzgerald.

"I listened to all styles of music. And I must be honest and say that in the beginning I used to copy their songs and sing like them. Eventually I had to decide on my own style. But it's very difficult to name one person and say *that* is the person who inspired me."

Mara also struggles to name her greatest performance to date. There are quite a number of shows that come to mind, for example the Royal Command Performance in 1975 that she and a few colleagues gave for Queen Elizabeth II in London.

"That was quite an exciting event," she says dryly.

At the time, Mara was in the musical *Meropa*, which showcased some of South Africa's most talented African dancing and singing artists. She had joined the show in 1973 on a nationwide South African tour before it toured Japan, Hong Kong and the Philippines.

Mara remarks that she has not experienced any major problems as a black woman in show business. But there have been some minor problems from her family. In *Meropa*, for instance, her costume consisted of skimpy traditional garb with a lot of beads. Her aunt saw a photograph of her, in costume, in the newspaper.

"She phoned my father, who is a priest, and complained that I had turned into a heathen." Mara gives a hearty laugh as she recalls the incident.

She dismisses the common perception that women in show business are of low morals. "It's not true. If I did that, I wouldn't be where I am right now."

The future of women singers in South Africa really worries her. "We don't give them many breaks." She feels that the industry itself, the SABC as well as the government owe artists a lot.

"They have no respect for local artists. They pump us with overseas music. They sometimes play Letta (Mbulu) here and Mara there, but you listen to their Top Twenty and it is all American music. There is no respect for us. I hope that with the new South Africa and a new government there will be room for them to develop the artists and give them the status they deserve." Mara's words are pained.

On the other hand, she cautions fellow songsters to look after their greatest asset, their voices. This is a problem in South Africa because "we haven't got proper schools to train singers.

"You get picked up from the streets and thrown into a studio to sing. After a few years these singers are finished. They haven't looked after their voices.

"I take singing very seriously. It's my job. My voice is my moneymaker and I've got to look after it."

Interviewed at her home in Johannesburg, in 1993

Margaret Singana (Mcingana)

Anti-apartheid activists more than the box office killed the South African musical *Sponono* in New York in 1964. Nineteen years later, explaining the musical's failure in New York, Alan Paton, co-author of the play, said it was not a success with the sophisticated black audiences because they saw one of its characters – a white principal – "as a creature of the colonial part of Africa".

But even though *Sponono* was a failure in New York, it offered a big break for one of its actresses, Margaret Singana: she won a spot on the influential Ed Sullivan Show on network television.

When she returned to South Africa afterwards, that TV appearance gave her a foot in the show-business door. She got the opportunity to hone her voice and her skills in musical theatre in the 1966 musical *Sikalo*, and nine years later, in *Ipi Tombi*, she truly came into her own.

The *Ipi Tombi* album – and Margaret's hit song "Mama Tembu's Wedding" in particular – was an instant hit and a runaway success. Music lovers immediately took to her and dubbed her "Lady Africa".

Her success solidified when, in 1976, she was awarded the Sarie Award, South Africa's equivalent of the Grammy. The same year her American record company, Casablanca, nominated her for a Grammy, making her the first South African artist to receive this honour.

Later the same year Margaret was named South Africa's Artist of the Year by the music magazine, *Music Week*, because she had stamped her authority on the South African market when her record "I Never Loved a Man" sold more than 100 000 copies and received a platinum award. It was also voted Radio 5's 1977 Record of the Year in the international and local categories.

Radio 5 rated her Top Local Artist of the Year and she made history by becoming the first African artist to appear in the SABC's music programme, "Pop Shop".

Tragedy struck in 1978. Margaret suffered a stroke while performing at the Colosseum Theatre, Johannesburg. But her music and talent did all the work for her, and in 1978 and 1979 she could have been named by SABC as Top Female Vocalist.

Courage and determination were Margaret's middle names when she made a storming comeback in the early 1980s, singing from a wheelchair before a sell-out crowd of 45 000 at Sun City, in what was then Bophuthatswana, during the tour of the American trio the O'Jays.

As if to assure her thousands of fans, she released an album, *Nothing to Fear*, in 1981.

As a guest artist with Hotline, Margaret in a wheelchair became a familiar figure at festivals and shows throughout South Africa during the next few months. She also recorded a top-selling hit, "Music for Africa", with Hotline, one of the top groups at the time.

A year later she took another direction when she released a totally ethnic South African album, *Isiphiwo Sam*, in the Zulu and Xhosa languages. The album won her two premier awards: the Radio Sotho award for best "traditional long-playing record of the year", and a special award presented by Brian May of the British rock group Queen for her outstanding contribution to South African music.

"Very proud of her African heritage, Margaret hopes that this album will be yet another milestone in the current trend of African music becoming much better accepted internationally," her manager Mike Fuller commented at the time.

In 1984 Margaret was again riding the crest of the wave as she collected more awards for her music and her contribution to the industry. She crowned all this with a memorable performance at Johannesburg's giant Ellis Park Stadium, where more than 100 000 fans and music lovers attended Operation Hunger's "Concert in the Park".

Margaret made another comeback in 1987 with the theme song "We Are Growing" for the SABC series, *Shaka Zulu*.

Two years later, when the series was broadcast in Europe, she became an instant hit in Holland and Belgium when the single was released there. Within weeks, the song jumped from nowhere to number eleven and then number one on the Dutch hit parade.

After four weeks at number one on the Dutch charts, the *Shaka Zulu* album stood at number 43 in the Top 100 chart of the Dutch radio stations.

Fuller said at the time: "Margaret is one person who really deserves a break like this. It has always been my opinion that she is one of the finest female vocalists to come out of Africa."

It was award time again in 1989 when she received the Loony's Award for her success in Europe as singer and co-writer of "We Are Growing". In 1990, she received the Gilbeys Music of Africa Award, another premier accolade for musical excellence in South Africa.

Although Margaret Singana is no longer as active in show business, and prefers to appear only in hand-picked projects, she has retained her wonderful warm voice and maintained her dignity in the face of what, to a lesser talent and a lesser human being, might have been insurmountable obstacles.

Compiled from published sources in 1993

Marjorie Pretorius

Two events stand out as milestones in Majorie's life: firstly, when she started out as a singer and secondly, when she got married.

Her career began in the 1930s under choirmaster J P Tutie at the American Board School in Eastern Native Township.

"It was the year I won first prizes for a duet and Xhosa elocution in an eisteddfod at the Bantu Men's Social Centre (BMSC). It was 1935."

After that she enrolled at the then famous St Peter's Anglican School in Johannesburg's Rosettenville. When her parents divorced, she went to stay with her schoolteacher father in Sophiatown. Later she enrolled at St Hilda's in Ladysmith, Natal.

She did not finish school in Natal and returned to Orlando East, Soweto, where her mother had a house. It was in this township that her fortunes would take another turn and start her on a glittering show-business career.

"I was discovered by Solomon 'Zuluboy' Cele of the Jazz Maniacs. After recruiting me, Zuluboy formed a four-girl group, the Harlem Babies. Our backing band was the Maniacs. Our regular venue was the BMSC, then the top centre of cultural activities for Africans in and around Johannesburg," remembers the 74-year-old Marjorie.

Working with the Maniacs, whose leader, Cele, is considered one of the fathers of South African jazz, earned Marjorie the honour of being the first black jazz soloist of either sex to front this top band. In fact, black bands did not use female vocalists before Marjorie appeared on the scene.

However, the Harlem Babies disbanded shortly thereafter. The teenage Marjorie did not stay out of the spotlight for long, because she was soon asked by jazz pianist and composer Wilfred Sentso to join his famous troupe, the Synco Fans, which he founded and had led since 1937. The highlight of Marjorie's singing career with the popular Synco Fans

came when they were billed with the ace singing group, the Manhattan Brothers, at the opening of The Rio, a plush cinema for Africans in Johannesburg, in 1951.

But the big one came much earlier. Around 1940 Marjorie became vocalist for the polished and much-in-demand Merry Blackbirds, under Peter Rezant, enthralling audiences in nightclubs and halls all over the country. They sang in Durban, East London, Cape Town, Queenstown and on the site of Soweto's famous Baragwanath Hospital, then an army camp.

"Audience response was fantastic. We played to full houses. At that time we had top stars like Snowy Radebe – impersonating the great American star Carmen Miranda – and Eleanor Oliphant," Marjorie's features light up.

The second major milestone in her life was her marriage on June 25, 1946. A year later, she says, "I had left music." Shortly afterwards she moved with her husband to Ventersburg in the then Orange Free State. Towards the end of 1950 she was back at her mother's house in Orlando East for the birth of her first child.

"Peter Rezant heard I was in town and immediately contacted me. He talked me into making a radio cigarette jingle at Broadcast House (the old SABC headquarters in the Johannesburg city centre). That jingle was the end of my singing career."

The major influence on Marjorie's career was Ella Fitzgerald. She, like so many musicians of her generation, spent

hours on end listening to Ella and other top American singers on 78 r.p.m. shellac gramaphone records.

Local musicians of the time who made an impression on Marjorie included Lindi Makhanya and Babsy Oliphant.

What does she think of today's African women singers?

"I won't argue. Nowadays we are exposed to many singers. But let's not forget that they have opportunities that African women singers never had in my time. My generation sang for the love of music. We never received any money to write home about.

"There was little money in the business. We were paid something between R8 and R10 for a show. For instance, I can't tell you what I earned for that cigarette jingle I made for radio. Even something like African women musicians appearing in films was unknown during our time. It was only later when Dolly Rathebe was featured in *Jim Comes to Jo'burg ...*"

But Marjorie says there were compensations. Hard work and discipline were instilled in her and her generation of African women singers. Especially when she worked with the Merry Blackbirds.

"Their pianist Emily Motsieloa was a no-nonsense workaholic and a perfectionist. We rehearsed at the BMSC in the evenings, four times a week. It was no child's play. I was cooked as a musician in that tradition of the Blackbirds' discipline," she laughs.

Marjorie believes that the attitude of the singer is all important. "I loved what I was doing and wanted to give my audience the best. Hence I did all my songs with feeling and understanding of my lyrics and what the band was doing behind me ..."

If you ask her if she were to be given her years back, would she be a musician again, she shakes her head.

You do not need an explanation to understand that she means "yes".

Interviewed at her Natalspruit home on the East Rand, in 1997

Martha Mdenge

The thing Martha Mdenge, a top fifties singing star who used to live in London but who returned in 1996 and now lives in Orlando East, Soweto, most enjoyed during a short, unannounced visit to her family in South Africa in 1993, was Thursday nights on the then TV 2 (African channel) of SATV. She specifically loved "Ezodumo", a show hosted by Bhodloza Nzimade and Thuso Motaung, that spotlighted the tapestry of African native song ranging from isicathamiya to mohobela to mqashiyo.

Back to 1993, when the interview was conducted:

"Mqashiyo music has always made my day. When I came back, I was really happy to find that it was the big thing. It reminded me of the Mandela birthday concert in London, which I was thrilled to hear," Martha says, the memory bringing a gleam to her eyes.

She continues excitedly, talking about her South African experience: "This is the people's music and I love the way it is presented. You can listen to it without tiring of it."

Martha, the girl who set African townships alight in the fifties with her hits "Mgewu Ndini" and "E-Jozi Kumnandi" and who went on to become a household name in the *African Jazz and Variety* revue, now confesses that she is a mbaqanga person through and through. This explains why, struggling to crack the London market after *King Kong* had ended its run in that city in 1961, she joined the Africa Unity Concert, a collection of exiled South African musicians in London, formed after *King Kong* closed down in December 1961, and who showcased music from the African continent.

Martha has subsequently made the British capital her home. She has retired from the stage and is now a foster parent to thirteen children. But she loves the current crop of black musicians in South Africa, and she loves their music.

"From where I'm sitting, I can say that they are doing wonderful things. These are the things which were lacking in my time."

Memories of her childhood in Cape Town, where she was born in 1931, flood back. Her mother sang in the Methodist Church choir and Martha remembers the thrill when she, as a nine-year-old, was asked by one of her primary school teachers to participate in a radio broadcast. In those early years she did not think a lot about music, she says. Then her family moved to Johannesburg and settled in Orlando East, where she started to hear the Basotho and Zulu musical sounds.

"This was when the community was singing at weddings. That really knocked me for a six. I began to put some names to the songs. And the ones that really excited me were mqashiyo-type songs."

She continues: "Those influences must have stayed with me subconsciously. My hits 'Mgewu Ndini' and 'Ibhande Ngelam' borrowed their styles from those early influences."

And of course, like many singers of her time, Martha could not escape the American influence. Most of it, she remembers, was picked up from the Voice of America broadcasts she used to listen to at night. Great American singers like Ella Fitzgerald and Mahalia Jackson added to Martha's vocabulary and grammar. It was this American influence that helped her when she worked with top bands like Peter Rezant's the Merry Black Birds, who specialised in American sheet and dance music.

Even when she was semi-professional and working as a clerk at Soweto's Baragwanath Hospital, and later as a reporter for the African newspaper *Bantu World*, Martha continued with her music.

"It was done for the love of it. If you asked me then 'Why do you sing?' I wouldn't have been able to tell you. But it was fun."

At that time, Martha points out, her main influences were the African Inkspots from the East Rand, Khanyi Mbatha and the Modernaires and Ace Buya, with whom she would later in her career share the stage.

The highlight of her singing career in South Africa was a concert at the Bantu Men's Social Centre in 1958. The star-studded concert to raise funds for a swimming pool in Soweto's Orlando was spearheaded by famous anti-apartheid priest Father Trevor Huddleston, and featured Dolly Rathebe and the Manhattan Brothers.

"The atmosphere was amazing. I remember seeing and listening to an astonishing musician from England who was playing the mouth organ. It was wonderful!"

Then came *King Kong*, and after that her career came to a virtual end.

"I've always been a mbaqanga person. A lot of Europeanised music was coming into the African market then. When *King Kong* came along, I joined the show and went on tour with it to England. It was a wonderful year in England. And I remained behind when our tour ended and the others came back home to South Africa.

"It was not easy."

Interviewed at Dorkay House, Johannesburg, 1993

Mary Rabotapi

Who could forget the Skylarks, the group founded by Miriam Makeba that ruled the roost in South Africa's recording industry with career sales estimated in the hundreds of thousands?

This was the group that, in a short three-year career, cut more than 100 sides, almost all of which were issued on 78 r.p.m. records. According to Rob Allingham, few artists in the fifties could equal that number and certainly no other vocal group, including the very successful Manhattan Brothers.

Mary Rabotapi, an original Skylark, remembers it all, though she cannot supply any hard figures.

"In our time there were no royalties. Only a flat fee for each recording. We used to get nothing. I've even forgotten what we used to be paid," she says dryly. "We used to be at a recording studio from morning to sunset, working ourselves to death recording our songs."

That, more than anything, explains why Mary left her show-business career after a successful tour in England with the jazz-opera *King Kong*. When she and a number of fellow musicians returned to South Africa in the sixties, she took a hard look at her life in show business.

The applause in music halls, their names in London theatre lights, over the radio, posters advertising their sell-out shows, newspapers, magazines and their names on everybody's lips – this did not translate into material success afterwards.

"There was no money at all. When we came back from London there was nothing for us. We had families to look after, houses to be bought ... Those are some of things that put me out of music." Her regret and pain are obvious. "Payment for artists was worse then, we were ripped off."

That is the dark, uncomfortable side of Mary's music career. But there is a brighter side. This is the side, she emphasises, that was, for her, heavily influenced by the American groups the Andrews Sisters, the Avery Sisters and singers like the British Petula Clark.

The talent scout Sam Alcock set Mary on her music career. It was a difficult time for the young Mary, who was hoping to make it to college after her primary school education in Soweto's Orlando and Pimville. Her musical background was limited to the songs she had known as a child growing up in the black townships. But Alcock encouraged her to practice singing and was soon inviting her to recording sessions as an observer.

Mary remembers those hard years: "There was no money at home for me to go to college. I was fortunate that Alcock started me in singing, and that's where I met stars of the time like Susan Gabashane. At that time Miriam Makeba was still singing with the Manhattan Brothers, as well as with her group the Skylarks."

Mary's singing fortunes took a turn for the better when her studio asked her to team up with Miriam and the Skylarks for studio recordings. Later Johanna Radebe was dropped from the group and was replaced by Helen van Rensberg, who was to be substituted by Abigail Kubeka.

The Skylarks that Mary remembers fondly are: Miriam Makeba, Abigail Kubeka, Mummy Girl Nketle, Nomonde Sihawu who occasionally added a fifth voice, and Sam Ngakane who sometimes sang bass.

It was an era of great music. It was a time rich with the music of solid musicians and instrumentalists like the late trumpeter Elijah Nkwanyane, Banzi Bangane, Chooks Tshukudu, General Duze and Saint Moikangoa.

When Miriam Makeba left South Africa in 1959, the remaining Skylarks soldiered on. They were on tour in the then Rhodesia (now Zimbabwe) when they were called on to join *King Kong*. Mary toured with *King Kong* nationwide for ten months before it left for London.

"I was among those cast members who returned when *King Kong* finished its tour in England. I had two childen to look after. I had to come back home," says Mary, who caught simanje-manje fever, the new music rage sweeping South Africa's African townships in the post-*King Kong* era, thanks to Mahlathini and the Mahotella Queens.

Looking at today's musicians, Mary is concerned. She detects a lack of dedication and a style that is heavily influenced by the "fast buck" mentality. But she is careful not to be totally dismissive.

Among the current female musicians there are some stars who must be taken seriously. Brenda Fassie and Yvonne Chaka Chaka are cases in point. "They have beautiful voices," she points out.

Mary is quick to explain that in her day as musicians they used to look carefully at what was happening in their communities. That, she believes, made their music relevant and solid, with an appeal to their audiences from all walks of life.

"For example, we had a hit song called 'Iyaguduza Lendoda' ('This man searches here and there') that illustrates what I mean. Nowadays it's a different story with most of our children. They are mainly after the money ..."

The words come from a the singer who has had some hard experiences in show business, someone who knows that money is important but can never be the sole motivation and consideration.

Interviewed at her Orlando East home in Soweto, in 1993

Mary Thobei

Mary Thobei tells the story of an ambitious teenage group which had an unusual baptism of fire in show business at the Odin Cinema in Sophiatown, Johannesburg.

Some of the big singing stars of the era were performing: Emily "Empress of the Blues" Kwenane, Dolly Rathebe and Martha Mdenge. The occasion overwhelmed the fifteen-year-old female vocalist of the young group, and she started to cry.

Her manager would have none of her tears. When the call came and her group stepped onto the stage, she took a deep breath. With tears running down her cheeks, she opened with the evergreen "Stormy Weather" – as if it was the last day on earth for her and her group. Within an hour the audience was on its feet, giving the teenagers a thunderous ovation. After the show an excited Dolly Rathebe went to the young vocalist and offered her congratulations and encouragement on a job well done.

That teenager was Mary Thobei, vocalist for one of the hottest groups of the early fifties, the Swingtime Trotters.

Today, more than thirty years later, Mary hasn't forgotten the spark Dolly Rathebe lit in her young life.

"To this day, I honour Dolly Rathebe for those words of encouragement and for what they did to my dreams." Other musicians who influenced the modest Mary during her formative years include Dorothy Masuka and later the Americans Mahalia Jackson, Ella Fitzgerald, Sarah Vaughan and jazzmen Duke Ellington and Stan Getz.

The Trotters' confidence was high after that Odin Cinema performance and they went on to conquer all before them. Performances included a sell-out show with another top group at the time, the Midnight Harmonaires.

Mary and her group then started to look for recording studios. Lack of a network in the industry proved to be a stumbling block. Eventually they had to record at the old SABC headquarters in Commissioner Street, Johannesburg. It was during these recordings for the radio that Mary and the Trotters met the late talent scout Strike Vilakazi, who took them to the Trutone Studios where they did some more recordings. But the group wanted a better studio and changed to Troubadour

Studios. This was 1956, which would mark a turning point in Mary's career.

At Troubadour she met some of the biggest and best-selling artists in the industry, including Mabel Mafuya, Dorothy Masuka and the sisters Ruth and Doris Molifi. Hit after hit followed. There were sparklers like "Baheso" with the No Name Darkies, and "Zaphalala Inyembezi" with Irene Mawela and Mabel Mhlongo.

It was at Troubadour that Mary also met the man they said had a sixth sense for spotting singing talent: the late Cuthbert Matumba. This led to her leaving the Trotters and concentrating on studio work with various artists and under different names.

"At Troubadour recording was a full-time job. Unlike other studios, we recorded every day because we had our own presses," Mary explains.

Her world came apart when Matumba died in a car accident. "I was shattered. I was depressed. I could not work without him. Finally, I had to leave the studio and freelanced with a number of groups and singers." She recalls some of the people with whom she worked: the very popular Susan Gabashane, Rosalia Moloi, Connie Motsumi, Nomonde Sihawu, the jewel from the East Rand, and many others.

When the auditioning for *King Kong* opened in 1959, it was obvious that Mary, singing with Mabel Mafuya and Thandeka Mpambane in the group the Chord Sisters, would get a part in it.

Although she got the part, Mary never performed in the show. She fell pregnant and was replaced by another singer, Marjorie Jordan.

"To make matters worse, my father died the week the cast left for England," Mary adds.

There was another aspect to a career in music which Mary thinks was vitally important for her and the musicians of her generation, namely the closeness between musicians and their communities.

"We had our own 'Special Branch', a sort of bush telegraph, and as a result we knew in advance what would happen in our communities, be it social or political." Mary smiles at the memory. "Take, for instance, the big Azikhwelwa bus boycott in Alexandra township, and the death of ANC leader and Nobel Prizewinner, Chief Albert Luthuli. We cut best-selling records based on these incidents. You would hear or see something in your community and the following day you would be in the studio recording it. We at Troubadour were ahead of the opposition with this type of thing because other studios didn't think like this."

But this community story-telling through music had one unfortunate and scary result which jolted Mary and her colleagues. When the legendary and colourful boxer Ezekiel "King Kong" Dlamini died in prison in 1957, Mary and Mabel Mafuya cut a hit record about Dlamini. Unfortunately this did not go down well with Dlamini's family and friends. As soon as the record, "King Kong Oshwile, Ma", hit the record stores, word from the men's hostel was out that Mary and Mabel had to be disciplined for their disrespect to the memory of their champion. The gang got hold of Mabel and she was badly beaten up.

But Mary, who was born in Evaton, near Vereeniging, south of Johannesburg, has only one real regret: she never got around to playing the tenor saxophone – unlike Lynette Leeuw who got the opportunity to play the alto saxophone.

"You see," she laughs, "during my heyday I hung around a lot with male instrumentalists, because what they were doing with their instruments was in a way what I was doing with my voice. I fell in love with the tenor saxophone, particularly with the music of (Stan) Getz. Pity I never got around to learning to play the instrument, just because the person who was to tutor me got sick."

Perhaps a big regret for Mary but certainly not for her many admirers.

Interviewed in Johannesburg, 1993

Miriam Makeba

Miriam Makeba is probably the most documented female African singer. "Mama Afrika", as she is reverently known, is South Africa's foremost musical ambassador.

She returned to her native land in 1990, and her story opened up the painful wounds which have been the lot of most South African musicians in exile.

"Nobody will ever know the pain of being an exile. You are always with them but never of them, no matter where you are."

Miriam was born in Prospect township in Johannesburg, but spent most of her childhood in Mamelodi, outside Pretoria.

"My childhood was not exciting because we were poor," Miriam remembers. She first encountered music when her mother took her to Orlando East, Soweto, where she stayed with a cousin. This cousin Zweli led a popular singing group, the Cuban Brothers, and Miriam was roped in.

"One day we were performing at the Donaldson Community Centre and the Manhattan Brothers, the most famous and respected singing group at the time, were in the audience. After hearing me sing, they asked me to join them. That is when my little career started."

At this stage, she also became one of the first African women to perform the traditionally male gumboot dance.

With the Manhattan Brothers, she recorded Mackay Davashe's hit "Lakutshon' Ilanga", which would become one of South Africa's jazz standards.

Miriam and the Manhattan Brothers were in great demand and touring was a logical step for them. In 1954 they toured the then Northern and Southern Rhodesia (now Zambia and Zimbabwe) and Congo.

When she returned from that tour, Miriam started her own all-female group, the Skylarks, which was set to dominate the music scene and record industry for some years to come. The Skylarks were hailed as the best thing ever to have happened to music in the African townships.

Miriam worked with the Manhattan Brothers and the Skylarks whenever they performed. All the same, it was a tough time and the money was not very good.

"We used to sing from 8 p.m. to midnight. In some halls there were no microphones. I had to carry the voices of the four men (in the Manhattan Brothers), leading them without a microphone."

In the mid-fifties, after the formation of Union Artists, a black musician's union with offices at Dorkay House in Johannesburg, Miriam briefly left the Manhattan Brothers to join the popular music revue, *African Jazz and Variety*.

And then came the event that would change the face and direction of South African show business: in 1959 auditions opened for *King Kong*, and Miriam got the leading female role, with Nathan "Dambuza" Mdledle of the Manhattan Brothers in the leading male role.

While basking in the success of *King Kong*, Miriam never thought that the songs she did for American moviemaker Lionel Rogosin in 1956 for his anti-apartheid film *Come Back, Africa*, shot secretly in South Africa, were about to close one and open another door in her career.

Rogosin asked Miriam to attend the film's premier at the Venice Film Festival. When she arrived in the Italian city, she found that after seeing *Come Back, Africa*, American showman Steve Allen was interested in her. He drew a massive 60-million audience across the United States with his Sunday night television show.

"That film was my audition to the United States," Miriam observes.

In London she was introduced to singer Harry Belafonte at the BBC, and he started negotiations to get her to the United States. After three months in England, she left for America. "All I had was my little suitcase," says Makeba.

Her greatest moment came in 1960 when she opened at the Village Vanguard in New York where she received "rave reviews from almost all the major newspapers and magazines". The four weeks she was to stay in the US turned into a year.

Later her daughter Bongi joined her in America. "I sent a telegram to my mother telling her that my daughter had arrived safely in the United States. The day she received my telegram, she died."

A further shock awaited her when the South African authorities refused to allow her back into the country to attend her mother's funeral.

"But the good Lord made a difference. I persevered," Miriam says of this dark moment in her life.

After two years in the States, she married fellow South African musician Hugh Masekela. The marriage was dissolved a couple of years later, and Miriam married political firebrand and Black Power exponent, Stokely Carmichael. That marriage, which lasted for ten years, marked a bumpy and difficult period in Miriam's career. Because of her husband's political stance, some of her shows were cancelled, and her records were no longer played on the radio in the United States.

Miriam left to settle in Guinea, West Africa, before undertaking an extensive European tour in 1982. While she lived in Guinea, she found herself cast into the role of mothering hundreds of exiled students who had fled South Africa. This was the time she became known as "Mama Afrika".

In 1990, when Miriam returned to the country of her birth after 31 years in exile, she said: "Finally, most of our leaders have come out of prison. To see Nelson Mandela walking the streets of South Africa, I went down on my knees and cried. I could not believe it.

"I wonder how the others feel for not allowing us to come back home for 31 years. And after 31 years they now agree with us that apartheid was wrong."

Compiled from broadcast and published sources in 1993

Nomonde Sihawu

There were few jazz singers in the country who could touch Nomonde Sihawu when it came to singing "Send for Me". No other singer could wrap herself around the lyrics of this song, put her own meaning to it and leave her listeners with part of the magic the way Nomonde could.

Nomonde, the 1960s nightingale from the East Rand, had served her apprenticeship in halls across the country and in the recording studios of Johannesburg. She loves to remember the great names and the various groups: the East Rand Sisters, Miriam Makeba, Peggy Phango, Mary Rabotapi …

"We used to rehearse in Peggy Phango's backyard room in Johannesburg's flatland, Hillbrow. That was before I went on to become the Woody Woodpeckers' soloist," she recalls.

Nomonde was the sparkle, spice and fire that earned the 'Peckers – Victor Ndlazilwane, Jerry Tsagane, Peter Thomson and Boy Masango – the title of the hottest and most polished close-harmony quartet that the East Rand had ever produced.

In the early sixties, the 'Peckers and Nomonde performed regularly in packed halls countrywide, as well in the former Northern and Southern Rhodesia. The only group which could be regarded as real competition, says Nomonde, was the African Inkspots, also from the East Rand.

When not doing duty with the 'Peckers, Nomonde was kept busy by stints with groups like the Hi-Lites, another top group. She also did studio work with a number of groups playing simanje-manje, which was the emerging "in" sound among urban blacks in the late sixties and early seventies.

In 1966 Nomonde changed her tune and joined the musical *Sikalo*, produced by composer-playwright Gibson Kente, who was breaking new ground in the field

of musical theatre that, up till then, had been the preserve of white South African writers and composers.

Nomonde stayed with *Sikalo*, which was bringing different and challenging areas of entertainment to show business in the African townships, until 1968 when "things collapsed for me." She is reluctant to elaborate, except to say that it involved her personal life.

Early in her career, Nomonde missed the chance of a lifetime: to audition for *King Kong*. In 1959 she went on an ill-fated tour to Cape Town with a group of musicians which included Patience Gcwabe and the close-harmony group the Lo Six. They were stranded in the mother city until eventually employed by the late Alf Herbert of the *African Jazz and Variety* revue. The result was that Nomonde was not in Johannesburg when *King Kong* was being cast.

"I was working with top stars in *African Jazz* – people like Louisa Emmanuel and David Serame. When *African Jazz* hit home (Johannesburg), *King Kong* had already left for London." Nomonde's features show obvious pain at the memory.

That was one of the biggest disappointments in a career that had developed from small beginnings while Nomonde was still a pupil at the African Methodist Episcopal Church (AME) school in Benoni's old Ethwathwa Location. She had big dreams about a career in show business, and formed a group called the Perry Sisters.

Her pianist-composer uncle, Labourman Michael Nzimande (who worked in a record shop), encouraged and supported her unconditionally. So at an early age Nomonde and her Perry Sisters brought joy to hundreds of people in African locations of the East Rand with their singing and tap-dancing.

It was not always easy. Nomonde confirms what most singers of the fifties and sixties say: life for an African woman singer was no bed of roses. Physical safety was a major problem, the biggest danger having come from the tsotsis, who regarded glamorous women performers as easy targets and harassed them in every possible way.

Nomonde shrinks as she recalls an incident where Susan Gabashane had to flee the famous Odin Cinema in Sophiatown when the thugs broke up the show because they wanted the singer.

Other nightmares included lack of accommodation for artists on tour, she adds.

Nomonde is heartened by the new crop of women singers. "I love them all. Brenda's (Fassie) hit `Weekend Special' is something out of this world. I love that song."

Would she be a singer again if she had the chance to live her life over?

Nomonde responds emotionally: "Even now I can do it. Ah, Jeanette Tsagane! We were together when we started our music careers in the East Rand. She was with her choir under Alan Silinga and pianist Jimmy Nkosi. I took Jeanette to Dorkay House and she became my understudy in *Sikalo*. She was the only one who could do what I did on stage."

Yes, she would obviously do it all over again.

Interviewed at her home in Daveyton, Benoni, in 1993

Nosisi Rululu

Nosisi Rululu started singing in the Salvation Army choir at East London's Duncan Village when she was fifteen years old. From there, she joined Eric Nomvete's band, which boasted top musicians like the late David Mzimkulu and Shakes Mgudlwa in its line-up.

"In fact, you can say they discovered me in that church choir. It was in the early fifties. The band then went on the city's night-club circuit with me as their soloist. I moved to Port Elizabeth after I received an offer from promoter Welcome Duru to work in that city."

She was working in Port Elizabeth with a number of groups when Alf Herbert's *African Jazz and Variety* hit town. She joined them without hesitation and worked with people like Clement Mehlomakhulu and Josh Makhene, who now lives in Britain.

"We toured the Eastern Cape and were moving north when we hit Kimberley. It is here that my tour with *African Jazz* ended. I teamed up with Abigail Kubeka and the late Dick Khoza and started a group. Our show was simply called *Variety Show*, and it did a brief tour before ending in Johannesburg," Nosisi remembers.

Back in Johannesburg, she joined the late Mackay Davashe at Dorkay House in a show which was preparing to perform at Lesotho's 1960 independence celebrations. Abigail Kubeka, Betty Mthombeni and Vinah Bendile were among the singers who spent two weeks in Lesotho. On their arrival back in Johannesburg, Nosisi joined the *Variety Show*, which was to perform at the Bantu Trade Fair (Batfair), and would afterwards tour to Pietermaritzburg and the Transkei.

Nosisi performed and worked with some of the best people in the industry, including the late blues singers Wellington "Count" Judge and Blues Ntaka.

"After that engagement I was back in Johannesburg and teamed up with jazzmen Dennis Mpale, Duke Makasi, Tete Mbambisa and the late Nick Moyake, who was then playing alto saxophone, Peter Jackson and Saint Moikangoa. It was a beautiful time of my life, working with those jazz giants," Nosisi reminisces.

She branched in a different direction in 1963 when she joined the musical *Divorce* for an extended nationwide tour. The cast included Mabel Mafuya, Patience Gcwabe, Pinise Saul, Thoko Ndlozi and Lylie Mtuyedwa.

When *Divorce* ended after six months, actors Sam Williams and the late Simon Sabela cast her in their musical *The Question*. But it enjoyed a very short run.

Nosisi's love for music goes back to her childhood. "I started listening to records of overseas artists like Ella Fitzgerald and Sarah Vaughan. But there were also South African singers, like Port Elizabeth's Mabel Magada, with whom I had the honour to work before I joined *African Jazz and Variety*. She was one of the hottest singers around. During my formative years I imitated these singers' styles."

Nosisi finds it easy to single out the greatest performance of her career: "Without doubt or question I will say it was when I appeared in the musical *Divorce*. But there was also another highlight in my career: when I performed with Davashe's Jazz Dazzlers. That band really brought out the best in me as a singer."

In the sixties the Dazzlers were one of the top jazz bands in the country. And they boasted top vocalists – in short, a vocalist had to be really good to be invited to work with them.

She continues: "I enjoyed a fairly interesting and great time as a singer with a reasonable amount of work coming my way. Until the new wave of music of the late sixties – simanje-manje, for instance – came onto the market. Things were never the same after that.

"But I love what women singers are doing these days. It is their time and it allows them to do what they are doing, but sometimes I envy them and think back on our days, for example, the problem of accommodation when we were on tour. Man, it was hard and painful! But we survived, because people loved jazz in those days. This is why I loved singing jazz.

"I grew up in a jazz tradition and it's in my blood."

Interviewed at her home in Diepkloof, Soweto, 1993

Nothembi Mkhwabane

Her Ndebele culture is one thing Nothembi Mkhwabane refuses to compromise.

"I feel a complete person when I'm wearing my traditional garb. I sucked my culture from my mother's breasts. And when I do this culture for my people, I become proud."

She has been called the "Ndebele Queen of Music", "Ndebele Music Sensation" and "the greatest traditional songwriter, musician and singer in South Africa", but it has been a hard, painful slog for Nothembi, who was born into the farming community of Carolina in the former Eastern Transvaal. As her grandmother was from the Mabhoko royal house and her mother a famous traditional dancer, their household was a fountainhead of Ndebele music.

"I loved music because I was born into a musical family. Because I never attended school and had no brothers, I had to look after the family's cattle." It was while tending cattle in the wilds that Nothembi had her first taste of music-making. Her uncle Besaphi Mthimunye taught her music on a home-made tin guitar.

After her parents' death she lived with her grandparents. When they died, Nothembi had to fend for herself. She got onto a train and went to Pretoria, where she found employment as a domestic worker.

"My life changed in the city. Somehow I felt in bondage. Days on end I was daydreaming about the open veld, my cattle, my uncle, my guitar and Ndebele music."

She discovered that her employers owned a guitar, and that they were quite happy to give it to her. Her life improved. The long, lonely hours became bearable as she played her guitar. Soon she was making progress. On her days off she would visit family members in Carolina and teach them the songs she had been working on.

"Then (in 1983) I hit on the idea of recording our songs. We would call our group Nothembi Nezalamani; they would handle most of the vocals and I would accompany them on guitar."

But it was impractical for her to be constantly commuting between the two points, almost 300 km apart.

"By a stroke of luck, in 1984, I heard that there would be a show at Mamelodi township featuring the Ladysmith Black Mambazo. I approached the promoters to give me and my group a guest spot. We were a success. That was my first show."

Every night in her room she would take a child's toy piano, her guitar and an assortment of traditional Ndebele musical instruments like the isidorodo, and record her creations on a tape recorder.

"I visited record bar after record bar asking for advice. At one shop I was given the name of a recording company. I approached them and we made an appointment."

A talent scout visited her and soon Nothembi found herself pen in hand. But there was a problem – "I was illiterate. I did not know what I was signing."

She did sign, however, and armed with a small keyboard she had bought, she recorded her songs. The album she cut, *Izintaba Azihlangani, Amathunzi Ayahlangana*, was a hit, but she never received any payment from the sales.

Her second album, *Ihlopekazi*, suffered the same fate. She never received a cent.

"It dawned on me that these recording company people knew I was illiterate and took advantage of me. It was then I decided to enroll at a night school."

When she showed the principal of the night-school her two albums, "she tried to investigate the whole matter but the people who made me sign the contracts were nowhere to be found. But I never despaired. Instead I continued with my night school. My eyes were opened and I even learnt to understand how contracts work."

With new-found confidence she cut her third album, *Iphathi Lekhethu*.

In 1988, her recording company in formed her that her albums were selling briskly overseas and that she had to undertake a tour to the United States and London. But she was unhappy performing in the United States: she was without her complete Ndebele outfit as some pieces got lost in transit. She nevertheless went on to thrill audiences in sold-out performances in venues such as New York's Apollo Theatre in Harlem and the equally famous Lincoln Centre.

The highlight of the tour was when she was named the first black South African to win the Woza Afrika Foundation Award.

In London Nothembi performed at standing-room-only concerts.

On her return Nothembi discovered that her third album had not brought in money either – the recording company was out of business. With the help of her night-school principal, she registered her songs with SAMRO (South African Music Rights Organisation) – from which point she was paid royalties for her music.

If the singer thought that her recording problems were over, she was rudely awakened when she recorded her fourth album. This time it was another kind of hitch, a deeply hurtful one: "The company wanted to change some of my songs. I put up a fight. My music cannot be changed. When it was released, I was not happy with the final product."

As her fame and demands on her time as a singer increased, Nothembi found that it conflicted with her duties as a domestic worker. Besides, a number of ambitious up-and-coming musicians were knocking at her door, asking for help.

"That worried me. I prayed to Zim (God) to give me strength to help these young musicians," says Nothembi, who has thus far helped eleven promising musicians break into show business.

In a voice ringing with conviction, she continues, "What inspires me is that my people honour and respect my talent. Everything I have, I must give thanks for to Zim and my ancestors."

Interviewed at her home in Spruitview on the East Rand, 1993

Patience Africa

Recognition of Patience Africa's talent came early. As a schoolgirl in Ladysmith, KwaZulu-Natal, singing at morning prayer assembly would not get underway before she arrived.

"My bus, travelling from where I stayed in town, dropped me at school only five minutes after assembly had started. I had this concession from the headmaster that he would 'hold the fort' for me, conducting a longish scripture reading so that I could arrive and lead the singing."

Of course, headmaster Reginald Goba had reason to do what he did. He was convinced that Patience would become a great singer. In fact, Patience adds, Goba was an accomplished musician in his own right and used to provide saxophone backing for her and others in their school music group.

So not many eyebrows were raised when, in 1963, she joined the cast of Bertha Egnos's musical *Dingaka* as a dancer. The show became a hit, but Patience's promising career suffered a setback when she married in 1975. There were heavy strains on the marriage of the fiercely ambitious Patience, who wanted nothing but a singing career, while her husband wanted her to be a housewife.

"We separated. And I went on with my singing. I never became a superstar as the word is understood today. But I kept at it because I loved to sing and entertain. It was not a question of money."

The following of fans she had built up refused to forget her. In 1977 they voted her best vocalist in a talent contest organised by the SABC among their top singers. The award was given for her moving and gutsy "Malishon' Ilanga".

Patience was the singer of the moment, and she also won awards in 1980, 1982 and 1985. But she was in for a terrible disappointment in the the late eighties when a new wave of African music swept the townships and her fortunes started plummeting. The trend was away from mbaqanga and towards youngsters like Brenda Fassie and Yvonne Chaka Chaka and the new sound that they were bringing to South African music – mass-produced disco music which took its inspiration from American pop and which soon got a foothold in the local market. It was called "bubblegum music" because of its instant appeal and lack of staying power.

Looking back, Patience is philosophical about why and how her brand of music lost popularity: "The country was in turmoil. For older people, in other words my market, it was a luxury to buy records, and they had neither time nor money to do that."

Quietly, Patience slipped into the cabaret circuit.

"I've been doing jobs here and there and in Swaziland. As I'm sitting here now, I feel young and beautiful," Patience adds with a warm smile.

Of course, she has not forgotten the sterling work done by record producer West Nkosi and the Gallo recording studios, and their part in furthering her career by encouraging her and pushing her in the right direction.

And then there was the American gospel singer, Mahalia Jackson, an early influence on her singing style long before gospel music became the vogue among black music lovers in South Africa.

"That," she explains, "is why every record I have made has one or two gospel songs on it. Mahalia Jackson made me love gospel music."

The highlights of her career, Patience believes, were each time her name was called to receive an award for doing what she has dedicated her life to doing. There were also tours that she regards as high points in her career.

"That is when people in strange places recognise you and treat you like a queen. Yet, come to think of it, I'm just a down-to-earth person. It is so surprising yet gratifying to see people put me on a pedestal, yet I'm just simply me."

The flip side of this adoration is when things do not go well for a show in which she is featured. Especially when a show is badly advertised and opening night is not quite what it should be. Those are Patience's dark moments, the trying times in show business, when her heart goes out to the promoter of her show: "Remember, to promote a show you have to spend money first."

Despite these dark moments, she is adamant that her work has always been meaningful to her and to her audiences and record-buying market. And that is what brings her fulfillment.

"My songs would reprimand, praise and pray. That is why many people haven't forgotten them – they were communicating strongly with my audiences. I know I have made my humble contribution to South African music. Maybe not many, many people took notice, because I was essentially doing mbaqanga. But I'm happy to see that the top group Soul Brothers are taking mbaqanga seriously today and, in a way, confirming what others and I have been doing."

These days Patience, the girl who came of age with well-known singers like Busi Mhlongo and Doreen Webster in Durban, says her big moment is about to come, "if I can find people who can look after me (musically) and take me to heart."

And it looks as though the pot of gold at the end of her musical rainbow is not far away – ask the sell-out audience that gave her a standing ovation on a memorable and historic Sunday on 28 March 1993 at the Johannesburg Civic Threatre.

The occasion was "A Salute and Toast to the Ladies", a nostalgic show that featured the music of the fifties and featured greats like Dolly Rathebe, Dorothy Masuka, Abigail Kubeka, Sophie "Sunshine" Mgcina and Tandie Klaasen.

With that show it was confirmed once again that Patience Africa's music will be around for a long, long time.

Interviewed at her home in Orlando West, Soweto, 1993

Patty Nokwe

In November 1992 the often hard-to-please Johannesburg audiences experienced an unusual show. One of the theatres in the Market Theatre complex was bewitched by veteran singer Patty Nokwe and her singer-daughters Tu and Marilyn, who presented the moving *Singing the Times*.

It was a show consisting of songs sung in a mixture of English, Zulu and Italian, and included the Puccini aria "Oh, my Beloved Father".

Each night audiences were taken on the nostalgic musical journey of a remarkable African woman whose experiences told of overcoming hardship and suffering to become an artist in her own right and an inspiration to people around her.

"I was born into music," Patty's voice rings out across the intimate theatre as her life in Natal's rural Eshowe district, in a typical African extended family with her father's four wives and thirty children, unfolds in music.

"There was this picture of my father and his wives as singing people. They sang in English and our native language, Zulu. Though I could not make out at that age what they were singing about, I promised myself that when I grew up I would sing like them.

"Well, God works in strange and wonderful ways. Here I am today, night after night, with my daughters telling my life-story through music."

In fact, it has always been Patty's dream to write about her life and how she became a musician. She had always dreamt that she would meet somebody with writing talent and they would put it all down "because I'm lazy to write, but love talking".

Then one of her daughters, Tu, also an accomplished musician, insisted that they tell her story in music. When celebrated theatre director Barney Simon came into the picture, *Singing the Times* was born.

Patty was just twelve years old when her parents, in accordance with African custom, sent her to Durban to live with her cousin and his wife who didn't have children of their own.

"She was little more than a slave. They beat her; at times she was green all over with bruises. She had to get up at 3 a.m. to fry vetkoek and then go out in the

streets to sell them. Then she had to take another box to school. While the other children were playing, she was selling," Patty's daughter Marilyn narrates this slice of her mother's life.

But in all those unhappy days music was creeping into her young life.

"There would be a 30-minute programme by the late radio announcer K E Masinga. One day I heard Mr Masinga saying that the SABC wanted a singer for a choir. That is how I met the celebrated pianist William Mseleku and broke into recording for radio. I was a sensation," Patty says in a warm, motherly voice.

This breakthrough into radio changed Patty's fate and fortune. She was approached by an admiring white woman who offered her training and helped to launch her into a singing career.

"She asked me if I was interested in voice training. When I went to her house, she offered to train me for free. She added that there was nothing much she could teach me except voice technique," Patty remembers Madame Davi, who was to thrust her into the wonderful world of concert halls and classical singing.

During the early fifties, the local Durban scene was dominated by powerful African singers like Doreen Mzobe, Mary Dube and Eunice Duma – singing stars who set the Durban City Hall alight with moving and spirited performances during well-patronised eisteddfods.

Doreen Mzobe in particular stayed in Patty's memory. "She could sing like a nightingale. I loved her and she dressed well. But she never accepted me. I understood that because she was a star.

"Whenever she came first in an

eisteddfod, I would notch the number two spot. And when she retired, I took over her number one spot," Patty later says in an interview, and reveals that her winning strategy at eisteddfods was to listen to the other female singers ahead of her and improve on their weaknesses.

She continues: "I had also one advantage. Because I was small in build many of them took me lightly. One adjudicator even remarked that I was a singer who was controlled by the voice. What the adjudicator meant was that I had a powerful voice and range."

It is not surprising that music lovers called Patty the "Marion Anderson of Africa", after the American soprano who was very popular among black South Africans in the forties and fifties, especially the mission-school-educated middle-class.

Patty recounts that tapes of her music were sent to the SABC with the view of broadcasting them on the former Radio Bantu. But they were turned down by a music executive, musicologist-author Yvonne Huskisson, who declared that "she sang too much like white people."

Patty, who describes her voice as mezzo, notes that the great era of music and concert-going, which was enjoyed in great style in the fifties, disappeared among Africans when the new wave music of gospel, mbaqanga and simanje-manje emerged in the sixties.

She is happy that she has been one of the midwives who brought classical music to life for youngsters.

This happened when her daughter Tu started the Amajika Performing Arts Institute at Patty's Durban home in the seventies. Tu's dream and contribution was to give township children something to anchor their aimless lives on. Something worthwhile – music.

Patty is optimistic about the future of music in South Africa, particularly about the role that black women singers will play in that future.

"The future of our singers is bright. It all depends on the individual singers who take advantage of the opportunities. Today people must know and understand that singers and music unite people."

Interviewed at her daughter Marilyn's house in Cleveland, Johannesburg, in 1993

Rebecca Malope

David Twala could hardly have dreamt that he was laying the foundation for his grandchild's future in music when he insisted that she join their church choir. Three times a week the young Rebecca Malope rehearsed with her grandfather's choir in Nelspruit, singing tenor.

"I owe a lot to him," the pint-sized singer who has become one of South Africas top pop and gospel stars, re-marked in 1992.

Rebecca's painful climb in the hurly-burly world of pop music started in 1984, when she had to leave school.

It was in that dark year that her sister Cynthia heard of a group, Dan Nkosi and the Villagers, that was quite an attraction in the sleepy Eastern Transvaal. The two sisters joined the band, with Rebecca occupying the lead singer's slot.

But opportunities were limited in the former Eastern Transvaal. Any group that had dreams of hitting the big time had to be in Johannesburg. Rebecca and the group made the move in 1985. Their enterprising leader, Dan Nkosi, arranged a two-roomed shack for his eleven-member group in Evaton, south of Johannesburg.

Then Dan Nkosi started doing the rounds, knocking on every record com-pany's door, armed with nothing but his group's music and big dreams.

In 1987 Rebecca met record producer Sizwe Zakho, who groomed her for the popular Shell Road to Fame contest, a project aimed at discovering and promoting show-business talent.

A polished Rebecca won first prize and became a pop sensation almost overnight. Since then all her albums have gone either gold or platinum. Her debut album, *Rebecca*, went gold within seven weeks of its release. Her second album, *Ma G-Men*, also hit the 50 000 sales mark within weeks. She has pipped other leading pop stars such as Brenda Fassie and Yvonne Chaka Chaka by winning the OK Bazaars TV Award twice.

At a Johannesburg function to launch her record *Buyani*, well-known musician Julian Bahula, who had just returned from London, could not contain his excitement. "This girl has an unbelievable voice. She has a rosy future ahead of her. I have been around and about and it's not easy to come by such talent," he said at Caesar's Palace in November 1990.

In 1992 an album containing only gospel numbers, *Rebecca Sings Gospel*, was play-listed on 21 radio stations in Ghana, Nigeria and Kenya.

Another gospel album, *Shwele Baba*, recorded in 1995, sold 100 000 copies in three weeks, making it one of the fastest selling records in South African music history.

These records heralded the birth of Rebecca the gospel singer – no wonder her fans quickly dubbed her "Queen of Gos-pel" – and with them she added another dimension to her singing-songwriting and record producing. Her songwriting talents are being showcased by the successful gospel group, Pure Magic, which doubles as her backing group.

It was inevitable that Rebecca would travel overseas. In 1995 she travelled to Israel, where SABC's then CCV TV channel shot a 52-minute Easter Monday Special. Before giving an electrifying performance at the State Theatre, Pretoria, in 1996, she had been to the UK and France. The Pretoria show brought a packed theatre, including a number of Cabinet Ministers and Members of Parliament, to their feet.

But 1996 was also a year of pain for Rebecca. Her father, brother and sister died one after the other. As a tribute to them, and especially to her mother, she cut another best-selling gospel album *Angingedwa*. It went platinum in only three days. Rebecca's record company believes it will become her biggest selling album to date.

In April 1997 Rebecca won the FNB South African Music Award in the category Best Selling Artist for her album *UZube Nam*, which was released the previous year. In July Rebecca and Pure Magic undertook a one-month tour of the UK, Sweden and Norway. At the same time, her record company announced the imminent world-wide release of her ten albums, spanning 1989 to 1997.

Said an elated Rebecca: "I never had any doubts that I would have a music career, but my success as an artist has always been beyond my wildest dreams. I thank the Lord for giving me the talent and ability to believe in myself, and I thank my fans for their support."

Today the husky-voiced Rebecca looks the part of a successful South African pop star. She owns a beautiful house and drives a sleek German car.

"Be careful. The music business can be ruthless and many artists do not survive," she warns young girls who have dreams of making it big in South African show business.

As Gus Silber once wrote in the *Sunday Times Magazine*: "In the real world, dreams don't come true that easily. Unless you're talking about Rebecca Malope."

Compiled from published sources in 1997

Ribbon Dlamini

Ribbon Dlamini's appearance in the 1951 film *Cry, the Beloved Country* opened the door to an exciting singing career.

"When the film was shown throughout South Africa I found myself suddenly in the spotlight and under pressure from family and friends that I should become a singer. I don't know why. Maybe it was my voice. But I succumbed."

She was snapped up by the Manhattan Stars, a Johannesburg close-harmony group.

When not working with her group she found plenty of work sharing the stage with top-liners Emily Kwenane, Dolly Rathebe and Tandie Klaasen. Her world opened up further as she toured with these top singers.

"Dolly and Tandie were marvellous singers. I remember Dolly telling me that she was so good she could climb a tree and sing and the world would be at her feet," Ribbon observes with a throaty laugh. "Those two ladies were your true professionals who taught me a thing or two about the craft of singing."

She learnt that singing was an intimate, personal activity. "It had to be as if I was singing for myself."

One of the things Ribbon has not forgotten is how she was taught to project herself on the stage. This was the thin line that separated the pros from the amateurs.

"To illustrate what I mean: there was this concert in Port Elizabeth where Emily Kwenane brought the house down. She was crying as she belted out a terrific rendition of 'Up in the Morning'. That performance will always stay with me."

Looking at the current crop of African women singers, she admires Brenda Fassie when she is at her best.

"I feel young singers like Brenda are good. Brenda, in a good performance, is capable of capturing her audience. That is the mark of a pro. On the whole I think most of our young women singers have a bright future. They have privileges we never had in our time."

Although Ribbon was a big star in the fifties, her singing career did not last long. A singer's career for an African woman did not pay well. Save for the glamour and an opportunity to visit and tour places most of them at the time only dreamt about, there was not much financial reward in it for them.

There were other difficulties particular to black musicians. Ribbon recalls an incident in Bloemfontein, where she and the Manhattan Stars were scheduled to perform.

"Hours before our show, policemen burst into the boarding house where we were staying and in no uncertain terms told us that we could not perform at the City Hall. Only later, when we realised that it was a whites-only venue, did the penny drop."

Ribbon wanted to quit while she was ahead. She hated the idea of going into decline without realising it. Her role as Gertrude the shebeen queen in *Cry, the Beloved Country* was the high point of her show-business career. Since then, she says, listening to the blues and American veterans Lena Horne, Ella Fitzgerald and Sarah Vaughan has kept her love for music alive.

She smiles as she explains her first name: her father died in January 1928 and she was born the following month. Her grieving mother made a vow that she would never remarry and that her daughter would always be the ribbon holding intact the love she had for her father.

Though Ribbon's singing career lasted a brief three years, from 1950-1953, her memories of her turn in the spotlight are happy.

Interviewed at her home in Orlando West, Soweto, in 1997

Sathima Bea Benjamin

New York-based jazz singer Sathima Bea Benjamin came back home in 1994 after more than 32 years of self-imposed exile, and again in 1997.

Her initial determination to succeed has paid off, because today the sixty-year-old musician is ranked among the world's great female jazz singers – an exclusive club that includes the late Sarah "Sassy" Vaughan and Carmen McRae, Betty Carter, Abbey Lincoln and Shirley Horn.

Sathima enjoys one of the rare luxuries in the world of jazz – to pick and choose her musicians for concerts and recordings. Any jazz artist who can achieve that in the tough New York jazz world must have something lesser musicians lack.

Her favourite backing musicians are jazz bassist Buster Williams, drummer Billy Higgins and pianist Kenny Barron. This solid trio worked with her on her 1992 album *Southern Touch* – which went on to notch an amazing four-out-of-five-star review rating in the authoritative *Downbeat* magazine.

In 1994 Sathima briefly returned to South Africa. Her mission was to bring a gift most South Africans were unaware of – to perform at President Nelson Mandela's inauguration at Pretoria's Union Buildings.

Said Sathima: "It was a great honour to perform for Madiba. I gladly flew from New York at my own expense to sing for this great man, this saint."

So intense was her resolve to perform for the president that when she discovered she was not featured in the inauguration music programme, she had to "steal" one minute from the five allocated to her husband, Abdullah Ibrahim.

Her brief visit inspired the wish to return on a national tour where she would perform and exchange notes with the many women singers who are scattered all over South Africa. This wish was partially realised the same year when she was the top-liner at the Johannesburg Jazz Festival.

Only a handful of jazz lovers were aware of Sathima before she hit the limelight in 1963, when she invited jazz legend Duke Ellington to listen to her husband Ibrahim (then known as Dollar Brand) playing at a club in Zurich, Switzerland.

Ellington loved what he heard and arranged a recording session in Paris,

France, the next day. The 1964 recording *Duke Ellington Presents the Dollar Brand Trio* is history. However, until 1994, when writer David Hadju discovered (in the course of researching the music of pianist Billy Strayhorn) that a duplicate tape of Sathima's 1963 recording with Ellington existed, few people realised that such a recording was ever made.

Hadju contacted Sathima in New York. This led to the release of the album *A Morning in Paris*, early in 1997.

Explaining her love for Ellington's music, Sathima simply says: "I have loved that man's music since I was eighteen years old. I never dreamt that one day our paths would cross."

In fact, Sathima considers a performance with the Ellington band at the 1965 Newport Jazz Festival, with the maestro at the piano, as one of the milestones in her career. So too was the honour to sing the music of Ellington and Strayhorn in the intimate Weill Recital Hall at Carnegie Hall in New York in February 1997.

Sathima explains her choice of jazz as the vehicle for her artistic expression: "You will not go to a thing if you don't feel a kinship with it. I come from Cape Town, music has always been a natural thing to me. When I heard that music (jazz), I went towards Duke Ellington. I don't do anything that is unnatural."

In the fifties, the birth of South Africa's modern jazz era, Sathima (then simply Bea Benjamin) was known only to a close-knit group of jazz fans. This included the pioneering Jazz Epistles, Kippie Moeketsi, the father of modern jazz in South Africa, and bassist Johnny Dyani.

"It was Dyani who named me Sathima, but it was spelt without an 'h'. He told me it meant 'a person with a kind heart'. Yes, I know that for many years my fans and audiences thought it was a Muslim name."

But who is Sathima really? She was

born in Cape Town where she also spent her childhood and formative years. "I don't like shouting about myself," she warns. "But I love to shout about things that must be changed. I'm not about me but what our struggle is about. Why should some people here live in First World conditions and others in Third World conditions?"

That explains why she is given to saying that her sister, musically speaking, is Abbey Lincoln, "because we write about social issues and sing about them". The same sentiment is echoed in her comment on Billie Holiday's work: "When I heard Billie Holiday's music, I was moved. She deals with the subtleties of life; she gets behind her songs."

Sathima's voice and style are unique in jazz. "Interwoven are a softness rooted in the singing of Ethel Waters and Billie Holiday and a deep well of passion: African tones, pitches and an element of Ellington, an irrepressible swing, a richness in colour, a subtle but undeniable majesty," the *Philadelphia Tribune*'s Jules Edskein once wrote.

In the New York world of jazz, Sathima's fighting spirit, her iron will and her dedication to her music have caused her to be known as "Samurai". These characteristics have helped her to accumulate a substantial body of work under the label Ekapa Records, which she founded with her husband.

Her followers will remember this label. In 1982 she was nominated for the Grammy Award for her album *Dedications*, produced under the Ekapa label.

Some years ago, Sathima described her way of working as follows: "You know I produce my music myself. I do everything for myself. When it is finished, I take it to a record company. They never tell me what to do. I'm not trying to make a million. If I wanted that, I would be doing something else ..."

The words and determination are true to the spirit of Sathima Bea Benjamin, the Samurai, who boasts seven highly-acclaimed jazz albums to date.

Interviewed at the Rosebank Hotel, Johannesburg, May 1993, and at Johannesburg International Airport, July 1997

Sibongile Khumalo

They say fate decreed that Sibongile Mngoma-Khumalo would become a musician. After all, she was born into a prominent musical family. Her father Khabi Mngoma, former Professor of Music at the University of Zululand, created a culture of music around his family and his Soweto community.

Sibongile, who studied music at the Universities of Zululand and the Witwatersrand, attended her first concert when she was just two weeks old. A clear sign that her parents would encourage her from an early age to attend exhibitions and concerts as well as to sing, dance, act and paint. When she was eight, she started singing under one of the most prominent musicians of the day, the late Emily Motsieloa.

When Sibongile finally hit the spotlight in the late eighties, a versatile and flexible musician emerged, with a fresh repertoire spanning jazz, African and classical music.

As a high school student in the seventies, she spent her weekends at the Donaldson Community Centre and at the nearby Orlando High School receiving music lessons. Saturdays formal lessons on the theory of music, drama and art would follow. On Sundays it would be youth orchestra rehearsals at the Centre. The approach was holistic.

"It became part of one's life. During that period it was like drinking water. You are not conscious of what you are doing, it is part of your life."

Initially, Sibongile had ambitions of becoming a medical doctor or teacher. It was about 1975 when she decided to become a music teacher. After completing her degree at the University of Zululand, she lectured in its Department of Music for a year before leaving for Wits University to do an honours degree.

The early 1980s found Sibongile a solid music academic. She is quick to point out that, compared to the risks other black female musicians before her had to face, her story does not include tales of gangsters and harassment.

She observes: "At the time, I was going on as an ordinary working woman. Mine is not a typical rags-to-riches story, I'm not even rich. But for me things fell into place. My experiences are such that it was not a tremendous struggle (to become a

musician). It was a decision taken and followed through."

Sibongile began to establish herself as both performer and dedicated music teacher and administrative worker. She slogged it out at the FUBA Academy in Johannesburg and the Madimba Institute of African Music, based at the Funda Centre, Soweto.

Then followed a stint at the Wits Business School, where she studied personnel management before she joined a consultancy. "After two years, I decided I had had enough of the corporate world and I knew what I wanted."

In 1986 she was back full-time at the Funda Centre, where she still teaches music and handles some administration when she is not performing.

In 1993 she won the Standard Bank Young Artists Award for Music, and that confirmed her importance in current South African music. In addition to the prize money, the real bonus was a concert on the main programme of the Grahamstown National Arts Festival, South Africa's premier arts event. That year brought another distinction: she was the only South African soloist to be asked to perform with the London Philharmonic Orchestra during its "Harmony Tour".

1996 brought another challenge. She was offered the lead in the Africanised version of Bizet's *Carmen* at the Durban Playhouse.

"Taking part in a full-scale opera is a dream I've cherished since I was a very young girl. Now that the dream is a reality I am not only grateful, but also awesomely aware of the great responsibility that it entails," she told the Sunday newspaper *City Press* at the time.

Asked if being a woman has hindered her music career, she observes: "I have been respected as a woman, but primarily as a musician. There are good men and good women."

Being able to sing and make music provides her with emotional and psychological relief. "You know, sometimes before a major concert you go through a whole spectrum of emotions. I end up asking myself: *Why am I doing this?* At the end of a show when people, the audience, appreciates what I do, I understand what it's all about. It's a gift one has, it's a gift one has to share."

She continues: "I find that there are other forces that take over (during performances). They give me the power to communicate."

Sibongile's parents have been the biggest influence in her career: her father has been her teacher, guide and counselor, while her late mother Grace, also an accomplished musician and a very dignified and elegant woman, was the stabilising force.

Fellow musicians Sophie "Sunshine" Mgcina and Letta Mbulu also influenced her. "Sophie became my mother. She took me under her wing, she became my mentor. Letta's music, her style, was a great influence, especially her early work."

On the topic of music education, Sibongile has emphatic views.

"I would say non-music education is a better option. The music education available at tertiary level (in our country) is an extension of the Eurocentric music model. There is nothing wrong with European or Western music, as long as it is contextualised. In our culture, we also have music education. If you look at our rural settings, we have songs sung by children, songs sung by men and women. And it happens within a certain situation: a thirteen-year-old cannot sing amahubo sung by the elders. We have to take those basic (musical) facts into account."

She argues that there should be a vanguard created to nurture black musical talent in South Africa. This would prevent some of that talent from disappearing into factories and becoming computer operators or clerks.

If such a vanguard could encourage the emergence of talent like Sibongile Khumalo's, the future of South African music is very bright indeed.

Interviewed at the Funda Centre in Soweto, 1993

Snowy Peterson

When bubbly Snowy Peterson (then still Snowy Gwabeni) went against the wishes of her grandmother, she was responding to a stronger power. That power, she swears, is music.

Her story starts in the West Rand township of Munsieville, outside Krugersdorp. That is where Snowy discovered and enjoyed the language and seduction of music in her church choir. But this joy was short-lived.

In 1955 she had to move to her grandparents in Newclare, then a "mixed" township to the west of Johannesburg. Her grandmother made it very clear from the outset that she wanted her to become a dress designer.

"Reluctantly I agreed with what she wanted for me. It was just to please her, though in my heart of hearts I knew that music and the stage were for me. So I was enrolled at a clothing-design school in Johannesburg."

On her way to work she daily passed one of Johannesburg's famous landmarks: Loafers' Corner. This street corner was known to the scores of Africans who worked in and visited the city every day because it was near the well-known Gallo recording studios, and numerous famous yet unemployed musicians used to hang around there.

The unemployed musicians were an everyday feature as they waited for job openings, mostly session studio work, at the Gallo studios. There was also always the hope of breaking into live shows, which were planned at the studios.

This very street corner would change Snowy's life.

Whenever she passed Loafers' Corner on her way to the design school, she would notice a group of girls staring at her with interest. One day one of them broke the ice and introduced herself. It was Zelda Malgas, one of the top singers of the time. When the other girls joined

Snowy and Zelda and introduced themselves, Snowy realised that they were all singers: Nomonde Sihawu, Zakithi Dlamini and Susan Gabashane.

"In fact, it turned out that Susan was leaving their group and they were looking for a substitute. They had decided that I would fit the bill. Apparently they knew that I was Snowy Gwabeni and that my brother was the famous jazz trombonist, JJ Gwabeni. From that day on, I never went back to my dress designing school. Instead I joined the three girls in rehearsals."

Talent scout and record producer Sam Alcock was very much in the picture, as he recorded many songs by the Hi-Lites, which now comprised Snowy, Zelda and Zakithi.

Snowy's popularity grew fast. The Hi-Lites were riding the crest of the wave, and in 1962 they performed at sell-out shows in Swaziland, promoted by the late Wonder Makhubu.

While the Hi-Lites were performing in Swaziland, the musical theatre in South Africa underwent a revolution, spearheaded by young composer and playwright Gibson Kente, with his musical *Manana the Jazz Prophet*.

In 1963 Snowy, just back from her Swaziland engagements with the Hi-Lites, was looking for a job.

Nick Moyake, one of South Africa's great jazz tenor saxophonists, who hailed

from the Eastern Cape, happened to be staying at Snowy's home at the time, and he introduced her to Kente. Snowy was on cloud nine.

"That show was dynamite. It was star-studded. The cast included Letta Mbulu, George Tau, Caiphus Semenya, Mabel Mafuya, Johnny Mekoa and the great pianist Theo Bophela from Durban. We went on tour with the show." Snowy does not hide her excitement when she recalls that wonderful period in her life.

After a year of touring with the show she had to return home because she had fallen pregnant. After the birth of her child, Snowy missed the stage. She did not stay home for long.

She joined top jazzmen Mackay Davashe, Gordon Mfandu, Zakes Khuse and Skip Phahlane in *Township Tempo*.

The show was short-lived and soon Snowy was back in the recording studio, cutting records with an assortment of groups. During these sessions she met other top-liners Pinise Saul, Jeanette Tsagane and Pat Maboa and with them formed a backing group who did studio work with Zola Matiwane. This venture, however, also did not last long.

"We performed at a few shows but the group broke up. By then (1968) singing jobs were getting scarcer by the day. I was fortunate that I landed a job as a public relations officer for a recording company."

Even today the disappointment Snowy suffered then is still apparent. But she brightens up when you ask her who had inspired her. With a smile that seems to warm her compact apartment in Western Township, she says: "You must understand that when I came into the music scene, jazz was the thing. And, of course, my brother JJ was my only inspiration and influence. There was nobody else."

Interviewed at her home in Western Township, Johannesburg, in 1993

Snowy Radebe (Mahlangu)

Snowy Radebe is an endless source of anecdotes. For instance, she tells the story of how in 1942 a white manager at the Dodo Shoe Company in Johannesburg would move heaven and earth to give his friends, associates and staff the chance to hear her and the Pitch Black Follies sing.

"But there was a problem. Our company was black and we could not perform before a white audience at the city hall. Finally we found a hall in Doornfontein, a suburb on the eastern side of the city. It was quite a big and classy hall with a balcony inside."

At the end of the concert, Snowy and the Follies performed a spirited number that brought the house down – almost literally.

"In that thunderous applause and wolf-whistling, out flew a young man from the balcony and landed on the seats below!"

Snowy's laughter fills the room. Shedding a tear here and there, laughing, she recalls the story of her life as one of the top female musicians of the thirties and forties.

Another anecdote involves one of her favourite songs, "The Mystery of Life".

"Because I could pitch my voice very high, I had this game I played with my audience, especially those in the front seats. It went like this: when I deliberately pitched high you could see their heads and eyes going up and up. Then I'd finish the song abruptly and it was such a laugh to see their heads drop so suddenly. It was as if they were under my spell." .

Composer, jazz musician and legendary *Drum* magazine journalist Todd Matshikiza once reminisced that though he had heard many great singers, until he encountered Snowy he had never heard "a voice of such great power, range, beauty and sheer magnificence".

Snowy's singing career started at her Eastern Native Township, a close-knit and lively community, then popularly known as George Goch. Snowy's public-spirited parents, as a matter of civic duty, decided to form a children's choir. The choir would keep the children in their neighbourhood off the streets and out of mischief.

This made sense, as children in the George Goch of the thirties had nothing much to do by way of healthy recreation. The choir, the Philadelphians, was made up of sixteen boys and girls, and won instant recognition. In no time it was kept busy

with singing engagements in the African townships across the Witwatersrand.

"We performed at venues like the Bantu Sports Ground in Johannesburg, with great singers like Solomon Linda, composer of the isicathamiya hit song, `Mbube'. We were going great guns," remembers Snowy who was then a sweet eight-year-old with stars in her eyes.

Unknown to Snowy, the leader of the Rhythm Kings Band, John Mavimbela, who stayed in her street, had taken an interest in her singing. He recommended her to top educationist-musician Griffiths Motsieloa, founder of the Pitch Black Follies.

Snowy's big break came when she performed at a Sentso show, *Africa: Yesterday, Today and Tomorrow*, before a packed audience at Johannesburg's famous Bantu Men's Social Centre. A star was born. Motsieloa didn't waste time. After the show he approached Snowy's parents for permission to employ her in the Follies.

Snowy, then twenty years old, became the mainstay soloist and actress of the Follies. Four years later, her career was somewhat altered when she got married to Nimrod Mahlangu. At the time that Snowy's first child was born, the Follies suffered a blow when Motsieloa died in 1945.

"The Follies broke up," Snowy says, picking her words carefully, her voice betraying sadness, "and my singing career came to an end. I could not pursue my career as there was nobody to look after my children."

In her retirement Snowy became an active member of the African Methodist Episcopal Church (AME). Again fate intervened. In 1955 her husband decided that the family should move to Durban.

There, feeling lonely one day, she attended a service by well-known evangelist Nicholas Bhengu at one of his crusade tents. Somebody in the congregation recognised Snowy. She was asked to form

a church choir. When it took off, there was no stopping it.

"Our choir was so good that we became a permanent feature in Pastor Bhengu's crusade work all over the country," laughs Snowy, who spent seven years with the church choir before she went back to her original church, the AME.

Again her reputation as a singer followed her. Time and again there were requests for her to sing in the church choir.

"I protested that I was old and my voice was old," Snowy chuckles. She complied but never again sang professionally.

In 1990 a sickly Snowy left Durban for Gauteng. Her children were grown-up and leading their own lives – one in New York, another in Umtata, another in Gauteng. Snowy was hospitalised.

"I nearly died. I was so sick that I lost my voice. Nothing came out, only my lips moved when I tried to speak. Thanks to the prayers of my daughters and support of family members, I survived."

Classical music was a major influence in her career, but South African and American names like Ella Fitzgerald, Dorothy Kupe, Johannes "Koppie" Masoleng and Carmen Miranda also feature prominently.

"But Mr Masoleng, my music teacher at the Follies, stands head and shoulders above the rest of my musical influences," says Snowy, who considers her best work to be her hit record "Isikhova" and her impersonations of Carmen Miranda.

Snowy, now a dignified 74-year-old lady whose features defy her age, tells you that she was named "Snow-white" at birth, but as she grew up and became a household-name singer, the name changed to "Snowy". Though she cannot show much in terms of monetary reward, she looks back on her career with satisfaction. Philosophically, she remarks: "I recorded many records. But in those days there was nothing like royalties. We earned something like R3 a record. Today our children are making good money out of their music. But there is a consolation. I always tell myself that we, the pioneers, were preparing the road for those who would come after us, our children."

Interviewed at her daughter's home in Benoni on the East Rand, 1997

Sophie Mgcina

A white lie told to Sophie Mgcina's mother one night in 1957 was the start of a remarkable music career.

It all began when she picked up a copy of the magazine *Zonk!* and read that there would be a talent contest at Dukathole Location Hall near Germiston. The urge to enter the contest was strong, and she was hopeful – after all, she sang in the Anglican Church choir of Alexandra township where she attended school.

Then came the white lie on the night of the contest. She would be visiting her aunt, she said. Her mother, loving and protective, had good reason not to allow her daughter to be out in the streets at night.

But that "stolen night" was to prove decisive for the young Sophie. She walked off with first prize after singing one song composed by the American close-harmony group, the Mills Brothers.

The contest was organised by Union Artists at Dorkay House, and the winner would be in a good position to launch a career in music.

As veteran journalist Basil "Doc" Bikitsha wrote in the Johannesburg *Sunday Times* in 1993: "Sophie started in the fifties as one of the best jazz singers in the country, and her contribution to the country's cultural scene has grown ever since."

The late-fifties up to the sixties saw Sophie blaze a remarkable trail in South African jazz. She was with the hottest musicians of the time, the legendary Jazz Epistles, that featured Abdullah Ibrahim, Hugh Masekela, Jonas Gwangwa, Kippie Moeketsi, Makhaya Ntshoko and Johnny Gertse.

This was the era of vibrant jazz shows performed at the Johannesburg City Hall and the adjacent Selbourne Hall, where Sophie and the Epistles took their art to ever greater heights. In the lull after the exciting big band era – influenced by, among others, Duke Ellington, Glenn Miller and Count Basie – had ended in

the African townships, the group found a new direction for South African music.

Then came *King Kong*. Sophie got a part and went to London, but when the show ended its run in London in December 1961, she opted to come back home while quite a number of the cast decided to stay in Britain.

Back in South Africa Sophie helped to keep the home fires burning, along with fellow-artists like the late composer-pianist Gideon "Mgibe" Nxumalo and Kippie Moeketsi, the father of South African modern jazz.

American jazz had a big influence on what Sophie and the giants of her time were doing. She vividly remembers the influence that Billie Holiday had on her: "I could identify with her story, the loneliness, the lyrics – it reflected the things that were happening to me and other (African) women musicians. I felt her anger. That is what I was interpreting in my music. I interpreted the fight that was in this woman."

Sophie was working hard, paying her dues. She was learning what she could from listening to Holiday and reading about her at the United States Information Service library in Johannesburg.

To the ambitious Sophie, Holiday was "a technician who could use her voice. And she commanded respect and she was black. That is what she wanted, and I envied and admired her."

Then in 1980 her chance came: she travelled to the United States, where she had the opportunity to meet and exchange ideas with most of the women singers that had influenced her: Anita

O'Day, Ella Fitzgerald and the grand old lady of jazz, Alberta Hunter.

On her return to South Africa in 1991, after a stint of studying and perfecting her skills in the United Kingdom, a mellowed Sophie said: "I'm now an academic. I know what my music is all about. I heard people like Alberta Hunter, who told me: 'Man, you can't grow old with that kind of gift (singing), you gotta share your gift.'"

This was after she had obtained her Advanced Diploma in Voice Studies from London's Central School of Speech and Drama.

Looking for avenues to "share her gift", Sophie became head of the FUBA Academy's voice and music department – a job she held until 1995.

There has also been substantial stage and screenwork for her. In 1983 she won an American Obie Award, while she was nominated for the 1984 Sir Lawrence Olivier Award for best supporting actress in the hit show *Poppie Nongena*, for which she also wrote the musical score. She was seen in August Wilson's acclaimed *Ma Rainie's Black Bottom*; in *Phiri*, an exciting South African musical drama based on Ben Johnson's *Volpone*; *Call Me Mister*; *The Christmas Story*; *The Lion and the Lamb* and *Holy Moses and all that Jazz*. Her film credits include Richard Attenborough's *Cry Freedom*; *Country Lovers* and *A Dry White Season*, based on the novel by André P. Brink, and for which she did the dialogue and vocal coaching as well.

But forget for a moment the awards and honours that Sophie has received in her long career. Instead, ask her about her career highlights.

"Having a job every night. Every time that I've worked, auditioned, has been a career highlight. There was so much competition and talent around. I had to work like ten black women to get where I am today."

Interviewed at the Yard of Ale Restaurant in Johannesburg, 1993

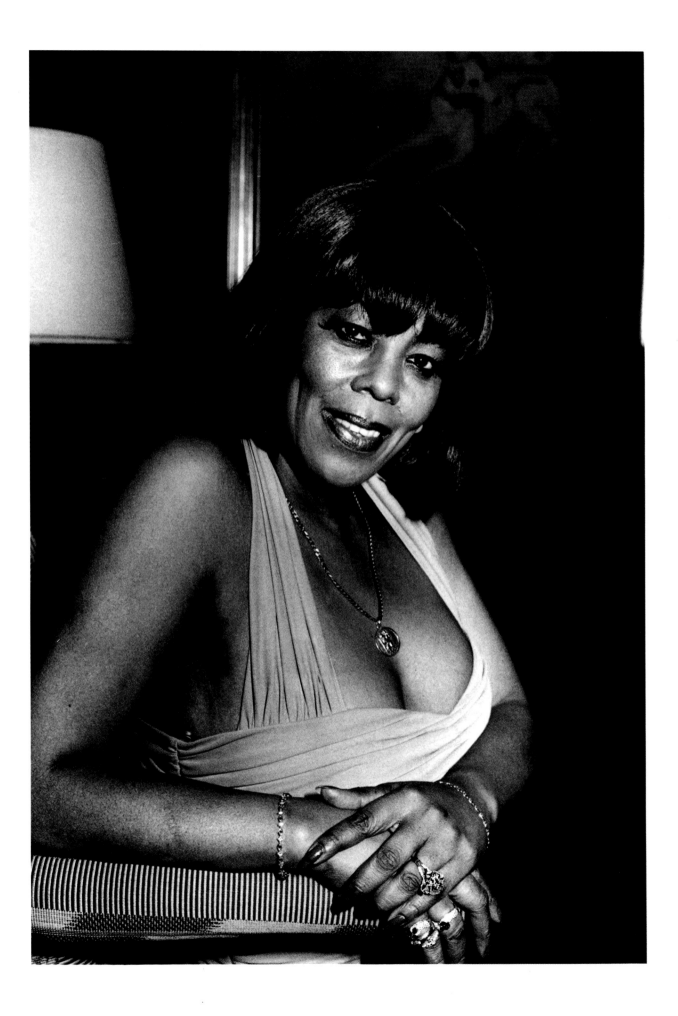

Stella Starr

One singer among the many stars performing at the Ladies Night Concert at Johannesburg's Civic Theatre in 1993 shone in an unique way. Her name – Stella Starr.

The occasion was to raise funds for the restoration of Dorkay House, home of African singing and acting talent in the fifties, that had produced some of the artists who were on show that magic Sunday evening: Tandie Klaasen, Abigail Kubeka, Dolly Rathebe, Dorothy Masuka and Sophie Mgcina.

For Stella and some of the older music lovers in the audience, the benefit concert was a coming-home affair. And two aspects of Stella the singer were on show.

Like her fellow artists, Stella, the ambitious girl who came from Sophiatown, had been touched by Dorkay House, but in her case it was not only as a musician. For Stella, Dorkay House was the place where she first came face-to-face with the world of show business. Dorkay House was the place where Kippie Moeketsi, Todd Matshikiza, Abdullah Ibrahim (then known as Dollar Brand), MacKay Davashe and playwright Gibson Kente refined their art in the school of shared experience. Stella had an excellent vantage point from her position as secretary for Ian Bernhardt, the live-wire impresario who made things happen and who launched a thousand careers.

"I remember when *King Kong* left for London on its history-making tour, I was doing the preparations for the cast, not knowing that I would soon also leave Dorkay House and the country," Stella laughs. "I had fallen in love with a German guy. And in the South Africa of the day it was impossible for us to continue our relationship. We desperately wanted to get married."

When Stella left her native land to follow her heart, she had only one qualification which would stand her in good stead in London: she could sing.

Her career in show business had started some years earlier when she was invited to join the Melody Songsters after one of the boys heard her singing in the St Theresa Catholic Church in Coronationville. For the young girl, who stayed in the same Sophiatown backyard as legendary African boxer Jake Tuli, this was an offer too good to refuse.

"We got a lucrative job at the top Johannesburg hotel The Waldorf. We did the clubs and a few jobs, like playing on Sundays in white suburbs like Northcliff."

When Stella hit London in 1962, she had little problem fitting into the English way of life. Ironically, the English way was the order of the day at her Sophiatown household where her grandmother, who was of Scottish descent, ruled the roost.

Then started a slow and steady climb on the London club circuit. Once she had established herself as a singer, she was offered a role in *Carmen Jones,* presented in Leeds. It was one of the highlights of her career. Unfortunately, by the time the opera got to London it had to be recast because of internal politics.

Another milestone in Stella's career was when she appeared in James Baldwin's play *Amen Corner*, which ran in London for the 1987-88 season.

A number of fortunate South African music lovers saw her in the seventies when she came back to her native land as a principal supporting artist on Percy Sledge's 1974 show.

But singing is not the only thing in Stella's life. "When I'm not singing in London nowadays, I do a lot of charity work," she says.

She is very active in the Lady Rattlings, an off-shoot of the Water Rats, who raise enormous amounts of money for charity as part of a long-held English show-business tradition. She has also been doing sterling work for Operation Hunger.

When asked if she was not perhaps thinking of retiring, Stella has an answer ready. "One of the members in my club of older English singers, the Lady Rattlings, is 93 years old. All of them are waiting for the phone to ring (with job offers). You never retire in this game," she says with an infectious laugh.

Stella describes herself as a singer who emerged from the Sophiatown jazz age of the fifties, marked by New Orleans-style community brass bands, American movies and fashion and a strong racially integrated community. She says the film *Carmen Jones*, featuring Pearl Bailey, and the legendary Billie Holiday were two major influences on her career.

"I cried when I listened to her (Holiday), morning and nights, in our house."

For Stella the secret of success is that musicians must learn their trade properly. "Unfortunately these days most don't," she remarks.

Her own music and career are driven by a simple philosophy, and have a very basic aim – which she states simply and straight from the heart: "I've always wanted to bring joy."

Interviewed at the Carlton Hotel, Johannesburg, 1993

Susan Gabashane

Susan Gabashane would have hit the big time as a singing star if a jealous boyfriend had not played a mean trick on her. She was on her way to London as part of the cast of *King Kong*, but she never made it to the aeroplane.

Before *King Kong* left South Africa, newspapers were already predicting great things for the show. It was going to be staged in London by the big and influential Jack Hilton Organisation.

"I and the others had our luggage at Dorkay House, ready for the airport, when my boyfriend asked to take me to the OK Bazaars to buy me provisions for the trip. We walked to the shops, which were on the same street as Dorkay House, but quite a distance away. When we returned, about an hour or two later, a sad Dan Poho told us the rest of the cast had left for the airport and that they were probably already winging their way out of South Africa."

On that day in February 1961, says Susan, something inside her died. She was replaced by Emily Kwenane, and the visions of a great career in London and beyond would remain nothing but a dream.

"I knew that I was alone. All my friends were gone."

It was a huge disappointment for Susan, the lively and hit-making singer whose career started at Soweto's Blessed Martin Catholic School three years earlier. Her teacher, Sylvia Moloi, encouraged Susan and her school group, the Gay Canaries, to record their songs. And when talent scout Rupert Bopape heard them sing, he knew he had found some amazing raw talent.

"He visited my parents and asked their permission for me to record for his studio. That is where I went with my greatest hit 'Skhandamayeza'. From there, I was in the big league with people like Elijah Nkwanyane."

There was a follow-up hit, "Kajeno", which according to Susan was built on a philosophy and ethic that have guided her throughout her career: think seriously about your listeners and give them what they want.

After doing some studio work, she went on an ill-fated South African tour which broke up in Bloemfontein. She was forced to join Alf Herbert's *African Jazz and Variety* revue, which happened to be in the Free State capital at that moment.

"In *African Jazz* I worked with people like Early Mabuza, who then played guitar – before switching to drums, which would win him fame later."

Susan's ill-fated tour presents a mirror of the difficulties artists endured in the fifties. They would spend weeks on end without pay, with the promoter pleading losses at shows. Then, out of the blue, the promoter would splash out on food and drink for his artists. On the other hand, Susan says, the tour afforded her an opportunity to work with her inspiration, Dorothy Masuka.

"She made me love music. I remember when I was a singing star at school in the early fifties and she would be singing her hit 'Notsokolo' on the rediffusion at home, I would be lost in her music and forget my school work."

The problems faced and endured by musicians those days is something Susan wants to forget. She tells of a show with Miriam Makeba and the Manhattan Brothers in Alexandra township which was violently interrupted by thugs. They demanded that Miriam and the Manhattans sing their hit "Ibhay Lam" more than five times. Eventually the late Zakes Nkosi saved the situation by convincing the thugs to let the musicians continue peacefully with the show.

There were also difficulties caused by the apartheid laws. The musicians felt it more because of the nature of their work, which saw them in the cities late at night. "But we found a way to get around the curfew (according to which Africans had to be out of 'white' areas by 7p.m.). We would keep our admission tickets, which would be proof that we were from a show. And the police would let us off with a stern warning. When we were working on recordings in our studios it was hell. Most of us from Soweto were forced to seek overnight accommodation in African townships like Alexandra because they were not so far from the city. At least in that way we could escape police harassment."

There was another problem for musicians: talent scouts did not want to see singers develop into composers. Susan charges that with some of her compositions talent scouts tried to muscle in on the creative process to make themselves partners to the composition.

But she doesn't want to dwell too much on the unpleasant side of show business. Instead she talks excitedly about those women and men who have influenced her career: "Like Dolly Rathebe, who was the queen. She was beautiful. I remember attending her show and admiring her on stage. There was also Miriam Makeba, with whom I toured a lot, together with Sonny Pillay."

Susan is intensely loyal. She was once on tour with *African Jazz and Variety* when she was called to Johannesburg for a recording date. Her studio wanted to fly her to Johannesburg, but she refused and demanded that a number of her colleagues be part of the recording deal. When the studio finally agreed, the group travelled to the Golden City by train.

What about the future?

Susan has twenty compositions which she hopes to record with a select number of fellow women artists. And the musicians she would dearly love to work with are Dorothy Masuka, Dolly Rathebe and Miriam Makeba. Because they would fit certain key areas with their musical know-how.

That is a collaboration eagerly to be anticipated.

Interviewed at her home in Orlando West, Soweto, 1993

Tandie Klaasen

Not many people know the story of how Tandie Klaasen made her determination to succeed as a singer known to all and sundry in London in the early sixties. Among those who saw the resolute Tandie jump on stage at that London club were popular musicians Johnny Dankworth and Cleo Laine. Looking back at that incident, Tandie says that it was all done for fun and to show that African women can sing.

She takes up the story: "It was during the *King Kong* run in London. Joe Mokgotsi of the Manhattan Brothers and I used to visit the clubs in that city, to learn and listen to the good singers making the club circuit. Then one day, we heard this beautiful big band sound. It was the Dankworth band. I could not help myself and I jumped on to the stage and sang 'Stormy Weather'. Johnny was impressed, and we became friends. He encouraged me a lot in my singing. He also gave me songs like the evergreen 'Cry Me a River' and 'My Funny Valentine'. I still have copies of those songs."

From that meeting with Dankworth there was no looking back.

As a teenager, Tandie's parents wanted nothing more than for her to qualify as a medical doctor. "But I couldn't see myself as a doctor. And during my schooldays at St Cyprian's Anglican School in Sophiatown, where I was a bright pupil and good singer, my father was broad-minded enough to finally see that I wanted to be nothing but a singer."

She formed an all-female group in the early fifties, the Quad Sisters, which also featured her sister Thandeka. The group was the toast of the town, and became the first African all-female group to make a recording: the 1952 hit "Carolina Wam" ("My Carolina").

"In those days, we played to full houses with top groups like the Manhattan Brothers, even challenging them in shows to see who was the better group. There were also good musicians like Dollar Brand, Jonas Gwangwa and Hugh Masekela," says Tandie.

Sipho Sepamla, well-known poet and director of FUBA, believes: "Tandie is one of the most underrated singers we have produced in this country. But boy, she is just greatness."

It was at the Bantu Men's Social Centre that Tandie got her greatest inspiration from the "Empress of the Blues", Emily Kwenane.

"I liked singing. I was impressed with jazz, especially during the forties era of Kwenane and the Jazz Maniacs. Kwenane was one of the greatest jazz singers in this country. We stayed in the same street in Sophiatown."

There have been others who have influenced Tandie's singing career. She names the African Inkspots, later Miriam Makeba and her Skylarks, and the Mahotella Queens, who introduced the sound of simanje-manje to the rest of the world.

Tandie cannot help but go down memory lane. One of her earliest performances was in 1947, at the official opening of the Donaldson Community Centre in Soweto. She sang with the Cuban Brothers, and together they brought the house down.

She also fondly remembers the popular singing competitions among groups, particularly all-women groups and their male counterparts.

"In those competitions, when it came to dancing, we would disappear as soon as the gangsters pushed their way in, looking for girls."

Singing has not always been a happy career for Tandie. There were the painful tours countrywide with no proper accommodation, and the numerous arrests for contravening the curfew laws of the time, according to which blacks were not allowed in the cities after 10 p.m. unless they were employed in jobs such as the hotel trade.

"We were arrested and had to spend nights and sometimes weekends at the Marshall Square police cells in Johannesburg. And all we wanted to do was to earn bread for our children! When you look back at those days, you want to cry."

She adds that she is encouraged by the progress she sees around her, and thinks that younger musicians are lucky in that there are now music schools for the gifted and ambitious.

"Unlike us. I wanted to read and write music but in my day they didn't have such a school at Dorkay House. It was with the help of people like Kippie Moeketsi, who gave us tuition, that we learned. I wish that our youngsters would make good of their chances."

Talking about the highlights of her career, Tandie recounts an amusing anecdote. She was appearing as a supporting act in Percy Sledge's 1974 South African tour and was grabbing the spotlight. After one show, the management called her and bluntly said: Please don't dominate the show. Remember, Percy is the star.

Tandie is as confident about the future.

"The older the wine, the nicer it tastes. We (the older generation of African women singers) are hungry. If Ella Fitzgerald can still be singing now, why can't we be singing until death do us part? There's also Sarah Vaughan. It's not age. Everyone is old as she feels. Age is just numbers."

She continues: "The public is going to hear from us. I am thinking of people like Sophie Mgcina, Dolly Rathebe, Dorothy Masuka. We are the singers who have kept the candlelight burning."

Given all the heartache and hardships of the past, would she become a singer if she had to live her life all over again? Tandie's answer is not surprising. "Yes," she says, "because it was meant for me. God gave me this talent. It's mine. I don't think I'll ever give it up. I'll drop on that stage, I'll die on that stage. I'll always sing, and I'll always encourage the younger generation that there's nothing to beat music and education."

How true these remarks, uttered in 1993. Tandie's latest record, *Together as One*, released early in 1997, features, among others, her daughter Lorraine, Ralph Rabie (Johannes Kerkorrel), Sophie Mgcina, Abigail Kubeka, Hugh Masekela and Didi Kriel.

Interviewed at her Eden Park home on the East Rand in 1993

Thandi Mbongwe

If some children are born with a silver spoon in their mouth, then Thandi Mbongwe was born with music in her mouth.

"I come from a musical family. My father was a pianist and my mother a singer. I started out in music, playing piano and guitar," Thandi tells you.

The young woman from Umtata in the Eastern Cape emerged in 1989 as one of the shining stars in South African show business. Yet not many South Africans in the industry could place or remember her. No one could remember a show in which she had performed. No one knew for certain where she came from.

Not surprising: unlike most South African singers whose careers started in their native land and ended overseas, it had been the other way around with Thandi. Her music career started in Canada, where she was studying in the eighties.

She tells how it all began: "I met up with Harold Head, a gentleman from Cape Town (the husband of South African writer Bessie Head). We discussed my music. It started humbly and we got a band together. At the time Head was bringing some avant garde musicians to Toronto. And he wanted me to front those musicians.

"He said it would give me exposure. He also got me onto the popular television show *Who's New?* From there it was all systems go. I played on though I was not sure what I wanted to do."

This was during the eighties.

She continues: "From then, I must say,

it picked up. And I'm not complaining. I went to America, where I met up with fellow musicians Letta Mbulu, Caiphus Semenya and Viccie Mhlongo, and toured the United States with them. We also did an African tour. Then I started thinking seriously about music because it was something I enjoyed and was paid to do."

In 1989 she was back in her native South Africa and, according to her, she "relaxed a bit because back home (here in South Africa) I felt that my style didn't fit the local music scene." But music-loving South Africans were lucky in that she cut an album locally, *This is Thandi Mbongwe*. Since 1990 she has been kept busy with steady work, which she enjoys tremendously.

Her face lights up when she tells about her early influences. Her music-loving family of seven played a big role in her development as a musician, and she spent a lot of time listening to her parents' favourite records.

"It was a happy house filled with the sounds of the Mahotella Queens, the Dark City Sisters, Dolly Rathebe and Miriam Makeba.

"As I moved on, there were people like Ella Fitzgerald, Diana Washington, Diana Ross, Nat King Cole and Barry White. That is where I found the different rhythms that excited me. In other words, I am not a one-type-of-music person. I think I have a wide variety of musical tastes. Like the music you will find in my house. I don't think you can hear it in our country."

It makes sense when she insists: "Thandi Mbongwe can't be classified as a particular singer. I'm not a jazz singer as many people think I am. I've never done a jazz performance but I can sing jazz. It's the African beat that gets me going. That is why I can move and expand into other African rhythms. Move from Mozambique, Zaire, Zambia, Côte d'Ivoire, Nigeria and Ghana. I can sing in maybe twelve African languages.

"It is the African part in me. You give me African music any time and I'll do it."

Her next love, she continues, is Latin-American music. In fact, she performs a lot of the Latin-flavoured music of Mozambique and Brazil.

"I've expanded through the years: I can sing Greek music in that language. I also sing Italian. My musical spectrum is very broad."

If she had to live her life all over, would she become a singer again?

"One hundred per cent!"

Interviewed at her home in Vosloorus, Boksburg, in 1993

Thembi Mtshali

Thembi is worried that South African record companies generaly are not focusing on local music, especially jazz singers. She charges that most of these recording companies are just out to make fast money.

"I don't think they spend money promoting our own jazz music. Every time you go to a recording company (with music to be recorded), they immediately tell you that it's not going to sell. They tell you this without even trying to push your music to see how far it will go."

When asked why she is fighting for jazz musicians, the answer is simple and straightforward: "I'm part of that group."

Sarah Vaughan has always been her favourite and has been an important source of inspiration. But there is a deeper connection with jazz for Thembi.

"Jazz has not always been American music. Most people who play jazz in the United States are blacks, and blacks over there are Africans. There is that connection between us and them."

Thembi has been involved with television and drama as well as singing.

After eight years in the United States, where she successfully carved a name for herself, she decided to return to South Africa in 1982, mainly because she missed her daughter.

The Durban-born singer has come quite a way since she made her debut on the South African show-business scene as a dancer in playwright Welcome Msomi's 1971 hit *uMabatha*, an adaptation of Shakespeare's *Macbeth*. Msomi had spotted her while she was a student at Isibonelo, one of Durban's well-known African high schools, and regularly sang in the school choir.

While with *uMabatha*, the drama was twice invited to London as part of the Shakespeare Festival. The exposure in England opened many doors for Thembi. When she returned to South Africa in 1973, she was snapped up by the famous South African theatre team

Burke and Brickhill to dance in the musical *Meropa*.

After the successful *Meropa* tour, Thembi blossomed in Bertha Egnos's musical *Ipi Tombi*, where she gave a five-star performance as Mama Tembu. She toured with the musical for four years, performing to packed houses in Israel, West Africa, Europe and New York.

It was New York, the world's show-business capital, that finally seduced Thembi Mtshali. She quit *Ipi Tombi* and made the Big Apple her second home. It was in there that she met ace musician and homeboy Hugh Masekela. This meeting resulted in a three-year artistic relationship. She was Masekela's guest artist in numerous shows throughout the United States and the Caribbean.

In the United States she also teamed up with another prominent fellow South African musician, Abdullah Ibrahim, and their association culminated in a number of well-received performances in Europe.

In 1981 Thembi visited Southern Africa with Miriam Makeba for a nostalgic and successful tour. After the tour, Thembi changed her professional direction and trained and worked as a legal secretary.

But when she returned to South Africa permanently four years later, she joined a top Johannesburg group, Peace, and helped them cut their first album. She also plunged into the cabaret circuit, starting in Swaziland and working her way to Johannesburg.

Thembi, who adores Dionne Warwick, Gladys Knight and Barbra Streisand, extended her career when she became a

television presenter for the show *Inselelo* on SATV.

More recently, she scored another hit when she landed a role in Steven Spielberg's *Deep Impact*. Filming started in July 1997. In the movie, which also stars Hollywood giant Morgan Freeman and top English actress Vanessa Redgrave, Thembi plays an African journalist reporting from the White House. Incidentally, Thembi also played a journalist in her first TV drama, *Phindi*. This, the first Zulu TV drama series to have been commissioned by the SABC, was broadcast in 1984 on the then Nguni language channel TV 2.

It is interesting and ironic that Thembi had not planned to become a singer until fate stepped in and nudged her in that direction.

For most African girls in the townships in the fifties, sixties and seventies, career options were generally limited to teaching, nursing and low-status jobs in factories. During her final years in high school, Thembi's heart was set on nursing, which was a respectable career among her people.

"Unfortunately I fell pregnant when I was at nursing college," she remembers, "but looking back, I'm happy it happened because maybe I would have been in nursing now, earning my living there. After my short-lived years at nursing college, I was on my own. But there was this burning ambition inside me that I would make it as a singer.

"It was a case of working on something I loved. Sometimes I would go for months on end without a cent for my work as a singer. But in that dark period of my life there was always the satisfaction that I was doing something I loved."

The rest is history.

Interviewed at her home in Bezuidenhout Valley, Johannesburg, in 1993

Thoko Mdlalose

H er words and her ideals make you sit up and take notice.

"I want to own my own record company. To run my (music) business and administration. I think I have contributed my bit to our music, though I've had a raw deal. I want to get everything back, I have been thirty years in the business."

Don't take this declaration lightly. Thoko Mdlalose has successfully written, composed, produced and released four highly successful albums in a career which has been marked by hard work, grit and determination.

Thoko was born in Greyville, Durban. Her father was a singer, whose forte was the ngom' ebusuku style, an unique blend of African rural music and urban influences which developed in the sixties.

She had a normal childhood, but one thing made her stand out: her love for music. She remembers that she used to attend the sell-out *Jazz Sledge* variety shows that were the rage among the coastal city's music lovers.

"One day I approached one of the organisers and wanted to know how I could become a singer."

That incident in 1962 would change her life. Thoko was subsequently discovered by talent scout Sam Alcock from the Gallo recording company in Johannesburg. This led to her leaving her hometown in the good company of, among others, Busi (Viccie) Mhlongo and Doreen Webster, who would also distinguish themselves as singers.

Thoko's signing with Gallo marked the first step in a long process of learning and fulfillment that would eventually take her to the United States and Holland.

But first she served her apprenticeship in Johannesburg, mostly working as a studio session musician with a number of groups.

In the meantime Thoko and her group, the Mthunzini Girls, began to make a name for themselves. They played at railway stations, entertaining the public with their mbaqanga music, spiced with indigenous jive rhythms.

Luck smiled more broadly on Thoko

when in 1970 she got sponsored to go to the United States, where she could expand her music horizons. She does not reveal much about the sponsor, save to say: "They were people who were interested in me and my music."

Her first port of call was Jacksonville, Florida, where she sang on the club circuit and taught African music at schools. Her big break came only in 1972 when she undertook a world tour with world-famous musician Mongo Santamaria and his band; she also featured on his best-selling albums.

Thoko has spent some time in New York and Los Angeles, where she did community work, teaching American children African dance and music, under the aegis of the California Arts Council.

She remembers another highlight while working in the United States. This was in 1976, when she worked with her friend, international mega-star Stevie Wonder, on a translation of a song on his best-selling album *Songs in the Key of my Life*.

In 1979, Thoko moved to Holland. In her new home in Europe she essentially carried on doing what she had been doing in the United States.

"I was received like a queen. European audiences will respect you if you come with something fresh, original and unique."

Things were looking up for Thoko in Holland. That same year she started her recording company, TNT Records, which produced her first album, *Malaria Fever*. TNT Records has a parallel company in South Africa, Dream Records, which at the time of this interview operated from her apartment in downtown Johannesburg.

With her band, the African Vibrations, Thoko has performed in Holland at night clubs, cultural centres, stadiums and African cultural festivals.

And she does not forget to remind you: "My band (members) are African people; our repertoire is African songs. Whatever I do must have an African identity."

She explains the African emphasis in her music and what it means to her: "It is difficult to work in Europe in the pop music scene. They have enough pop stars. They see us as African musicians who must play African music. You must have your African roots so that audiences respect and give you support."

South African musicians Miriam Makeba, the Dark City Sisters and "kwela king" Spokes Mashiyane and his "crown prince" Lemmy Mabaso stand out as Thoko's major musical inspiration.

"Especially when I was growing up in Durban. There was a good, trusted gramophone at home. That was my first contact with those wonderful and talented musicians who were such an inspiration to me."

What about the future? A deadpan Thoko tells you that we must give it time. But she is happy that the new generation of African women singers in her country are "far better educated about the industry.

"Now we are going to talk business. Now our people are more professional though we were disadvantaged (to begin with). We have shown that we have talent and feeling for what we do."

This is the mature Thoko, whom a number of lucky music lovers enjoyed in Johannesburg in July 1996 when she kicked off the *Tribute to Africa's Women of Song* concert series at Kippie's Jazz Club in Johannesburg.

This is Thoko Mdlalose, one of the truly talented entertainers South Africa has produced. She has achieved success in her own country and in the competitive international market, where only the strong survive.

Interviewed at her home in downtown Johannesburg in 1993

Thoko Ndlozi

Thoko Ndlozi's mother never dreamt that her singer-friend Mabel Mafuya, one of the hottest African stars of the 1950s, had had such an overpowering influence on her daughter. "Mafuya was a close friend of my mother and at the time she was recording hits like 'Tickey-a-Kiss'. That was when I decided that I would take up singing," Thoko remembers.

During her schooldays at one of Johannesburg's old mining villages, Crown Mines, Thoko discovered that she had the talent to do so. Besides, she had heard and loved the music of black American stars like Ella Fitzgerald, Gladys Knight and Dinah Washington. But her apprenticeship she served in school plays and end-of-the-year concerts.

When Thoko left school in 1961, she joined a road show, *Uncle Joe's Rhythm Cabins*. But tragedy struck the show after seven months when its founder died. In the meantime she had also had a role in *Divorce*, a play by Oswald Mtshali, directed by the late screen star Simon Mabhunu Sabela, which folded in 1963 after just a few months.

It was only in 1968 when she started to work with Gibson Kente that music lovers really began to notice Thoko. She performed in *Sikalo* and *Zwi*, which became the rave of the townships in the seventies as theatre, particularly musicals, gripped the imaginations of urban black audiences.

From musical theatre Thoko became a member of a female singing quartet in 1971. The quartet, the name of which she cannot recall, featured Pinky Mseleku, now in London, Petunia Mabuya, now in Germany, and Audrey Motaung. It was aiming high and had its sights on a backing spot for American singer Brook Brenton, who was touring South Africa at the time.

Unfortunately another female group ended up backing the American singer, and Thoko's quartet undertook a tour to the then Rhodesia with guitarist John Nyathi instead.

When she came back home, there was nothing much happening except at Soweto's Pelican Club, where Thoko made guest appearances for almost a year. After this she was offered a cabaret stint at Swaziland's Penguin Club. She did reasonably well. This was followed by a short cabaret run at the Tamila Club in the then Lourenço Marques, now Maputo.

Thoko's career was moving at a slow but assured pace. When she returned from Mozambique, she joined Dave Bestman on a South African tour with the Coon Carnival Show from Cape Town. Again it was back to the club circuit for Thoko. But this time it was at a new club, Lovers Fantasy, in Johannesburg and her old haunt, The Pelican in Soweto.

"I was doing two clubs at the time. One evening at Lovers Fantasy Ian Bernhardt spotted me. An excited Bernhardt told me he had an idea for a ladies trio but he didn't know who to get. And he was convinced that I fitted his ideas and plans."

Enter Anneline Malebu and Felicia Marion and one of South Africa's most exciting female trio's was born: Joy, whose music would add an unheard-of sophistication to African singing. As soon as Joy came with its first hit, "Ain't Gonna Stop till I Get to the Top", it was the group of the moment.

The song caught the mood of the time, especially in Johannesburg, Soweto and the East Rand, where clubs were the big thing and establishments like The Pelican, The New York City and The Forest were barometers of the vibe.

Joy's biggest hit, "Paradise Road", was the highlight of Thoko's career. She had arrived.

The time with Joy gave her a chance to express herself as a musician. She explains: "I always wanted to make sure that the message I deliver through song reaches the audience. Fortunately for us the songs we did as Joy had so much meaning, talking to people, giving them hope that one day they will be walking through 'Paradise Road'. I always express myself in a way that people in the audience get the message.".

Today Thoko, who is kept busy doing live shows with Miriam Makeba, is still a bright and hungry musician. She is driven by a dream one day to represent all that is good in African South African women singers.

Interviewed at her home in Dube Village, Soweto, 1993

Thoko Thomo

When interviewed in 1993, Thoko "Shukuma" Thomo, a sizzling star at the pinnacle of her career in the fifties, looked back and compared her era with today. It was not obvious then that she was suffering from an illness that would finally claim her in mid-1995.

But let's turn the clock back to 1993: "Imagine if there had been television in the fifties. My children would know what I mean when I say 'I was hot'. I never played games on that stage."As a young girl, Thoko initially earned her living as a factory machinist in Doornfontein, Johannesburg's clothing factory district.

At knock-off time every weekday, she would rush home in Eastern Native Township – popularly known then as George Goch – and, after a quick change of clothing and a cup of tea, storm to the local Salvation Army Hall to meet her group, the popular Lo Six, for rehearsals.

"Every day of the week we would keep that rigorous rehearsal schedule. On weekends we would be performing," explains Thoko, who was nicknamed "Shukuma" ("Shake" in English) by loving fans and her proud community.

Becoming a singer transformed her from a typical, shy African girl from the township into a household name, someone who would later be used to advertise products – from cigarettes, chocolates and floor polish to skin-lightening cream. Yet all she loved to do in the beginning was sing at school and in her Bantu Methodist Church choir.

Occasionally her teacher, Matome Ramogopa, who was also a musician, would organise concerts with church choirs. Thoko remembers this period as an exciting time in her life, and singing the Handel's *Hallelujah Chorus* as thrilling.

But Ramogopa had a special interest in her as a singer. He was forever pleading with her to join his group, the Lo Six, as a vocalist. He even approached Thoko's parents.

"My parents flatly refused to let me join his group. Their argument was that a singing career would take me out of church. Another reason was that they, like most parents at the time, took a dim view of women singers. They told him that a music career would corrupt me and that I would be naughty," Thoko laughs.

But her teacher was a persistent man. He kept pleading with her and her parents. Finally Ramogopa's persistence paid off – her parents gave their permission and a new world of bright lights and music opened for Thoko, the shy and reserved singing star of the Bantu Methodist Church.

As though this was a cue for greater things to happen, the Lo Six with their brand new vocalist burst onto the market with a hit called "Thoko Shukuma", composed by Ramogopa. A star was born.

"'Shukuma' is the record which made me famous. It was an amazing hit. Suddenly we were in big demand. We went on a countrywide tour."

When she and the Lo Six hit the limelight, it was a rough time for most African female singers generally. Gangsters regarded them as easy prey, and many singers were forced to become the gangsters' lovers. Not Thoko.

"Maybe because I was a shy girl. I was lucky that tsotsis never troubled me. When things became hot for women singers during and after shows, the tsotsis would put me into a car to take me home with the words: 'You sang well, now go home.' That was our life."

She continues: "Then came *Township Jazz* in 1955 under Ian Bernhardt, who was impressed by the Lo Six and myself.

It was a great moment in my career when I performed with giants of the time like Ben 'Satch' Masinga, Letta Mbulu, Sophie Mgcina, Miriam Makeba and the Manhattan Brothers."

But circumstances beyond Thoko's control prevented her from striking the big time: family commitments made it impossible for her to audition for the jazz opera *King Kong* in 1959. The Lo Six, who also did not make it for *King Kong*, left for Kenya instead of London.

"I did a lot of freelance work then. Some of the musicians with whom I worked included Zakes Nkosi and Ntemi Piliso, who taught me a lot about being a soloist. On the other hand, I was listening to great overseas singers like Ella Fitzgerald and Sarah Vaughan, and learning a lot from them as well."

She has not forgotten one special person who helped in her grow as a singer – Kippie Moeketsi, her occasional mentor and the father of modern South African jazz, who also stayed in Eastern Native township.

"We had toured with him and at one time he was in my backing band. Kippie gave me valuable tips about my music."

She carefully considers her words when you ask her to name the influences in her career. "We loved music at home. When we relaxed, we sang. But I also loved Dolly Rathebe and Tandie Klaasen. I remember I was about nineteen years old when I attended their show at the Bantu Men's Social Centre in Johannesburg and I just knew that music was also for me."

She does not hesitate when asked about her career highlights. "The *African Jazz and Variety*, especially at Johannesburg's Selbourne Hall, were the greatest shows in my career."

Thoko Thomo is convinced that she could have achieved much as a musician, but marriage and its commitments have prevented her from spending more time on her first love: her music.

Interviewed at her Soweto home in 1993

Thuli Dumakude

Talk of dynamite coming in small packages! Thuli Dumakude fits the bill perfectly. She describes herself as "a lady from Durban who is a singer and a choreographer," and she quickly tells you that her priority is music. She prides herself on a natural singing voice, adding that she was never professionally trained.

Yet her voice has a quality and drama that never fails to move listeners.

In Richard Attenborough's *Cry Freedom*, Thuli's voice stood out in two songs, "Nkosi Sikelel' iAfrika", in a scene depicting Biko's funeral, and "Soweto", in which she was joined by the children from Bulawayo and Lobengula in Zimbabwe.

But it was her album, recorded in the United States in 1992, which pre-occupied Thuli at the time of this interview. The album, *Senzeni Na?*, had been building inside her for the previous ten years. It was forged on the anvil of the violence which had been wreaking havoc in her homeland, South Africa.

Living in New York has given her a critical perspective on South Africa. This caused her to take a hard and cold look at her native land, particularly the violence that has been tearing apart the African communities in general and Natal in particular before – and after – the political change-over in 1994.

Her favourite track on the album *Nkosi Yami* laments the loss of individual liberty, human dignity and respect for the sanctity of life. It is a vision inspired by film clips she saw in New York in 1992, showing the violence in South Africa at the time.

One specific frame struck a chord in her. It showed an African boy – maybe seventeen years old – gunned down in cold blood while he was crossing a street in one of the townships.

Thuli says it was at that chilling moment, as she watched the boy's life ebb away, that she heard a voice in her imagination screaming: "Nkosikodwa ngenzeni na?" ("Lord, what have I done?"). This basically explains her album, which she considers a milestone in her career. It is a prayer for peace in her troubled native land.

She cannot hide her pain: "Our children are dying; our fathers are killing each other. Now my question is: Why? What have we done? Has something gone wrong with us as a people?"

Thuli could be described as a child of the South African music revolution. She won her spurs with an electric performance in the South African musical drama *Poppie Nongena*, for which she received one of Britain's most coveted theatre awards, the Lawrence Olivier, in 1984.

Thuli's only remark at the time was: "Now I have graduated."

The acclaim she won for *Poppie Nongena* confirmed her remarkable talent. At last she had arrived in one of the most taxing environments in the world of show business – London.

"What more could I ask for? I was among the big ones in London. In fact, the news came to me in South Africa. I had decided not to be in London when the winner was announced. When my producer called me at home and told me that I had won the award, I was screaming at the top of my voice.

"It became such a personal victory. Firstly, because I am a black woman. I remember my producer asking what he should say in his acceptance speech. I said he must say I dedicate the award to all black women in South Africa. As you know, the play is about an African domestic in South Africa.

"In spite of the red tape of pass books and permits, she (Poppie) made sure that she fed her children. She was also abused in the process. That is why I felt so good in winning that award and portraying her the best I could."

Thuli related strongly to the story of *Poppie Nongena* (based on the novel by Afrikaans author Elsa Joubert). As a singer-actress in South Africa, she also had a hard and long journey to make.

In the seventies she won first prize in a music contest that featured top musicians like Margaret Singana. But she became a household name when she featured in *uMabatha*, the Zulu translation of Shakespeare's *Macbeth*, which won critical acclaim in South Africa and Britain.

Thuli has been blessed with a strong family support system. When she was growing up, her home in Durban was full of music. Her biggest influence was her mother, who was popular as a singer in their local church. It is no wonder that Thuli's family eventually formed a family choir that entertained at birthday parties and weddings in the black townships in and around the coastal city.

Beyond the family circle, one of her greatest influences was "Mama Afrika", Miriam Makeba. While growing up in Durban in the fifties and early sixties, Thuli would listen to Makeba's records attentively.

"I would imitate her songs. Slowly I began to find myself, find my voice and develop it. I remember those days – all I wanted was to hear her voice on the radio. It was such a loss to me when she left South Africa in 1959."

But Thuli is thankful for those early music lessons she learnt from her family and from imitating singers like Miriam Makeba. Years later, when she was to perform in the United States, those humble lessons stood her in good stead.

Thuli will come back to South Africa, this time for good. She believes she has a responsibility to teach those who will come after her.

"I am coming back home to teach. I want to come back as a productive African in the musical field. I would like to participate at the FUBA Academy in Johannesburg or some such music institution in South Africa. Or become a vocal coach teaching our young people what the voice is all about."

Interviewed at the Cleveland home of singer Marilyn Nokwe in Johannesburg, 1993

Tu Nokwe

As a young woman Tu Nokwe flew all the way from her home in KwaMashu, Durban, to England for an audition at an opera school. This was in 1985.

"I wanted to challenge myself. I wanted to see if I could stand on my own," says Tu.

In London she was fortunate. Everywhere she went, musicians were eager to work with her. But her mission was an audition at an opera school.

She passed the audition with flying colours, but she could not enroll at the school for various reasons, one being financial.

"I was in a fix until fellow South African musician Julian Bahula employed me at his Club 100. But I did not like London, so I returned to Durban."

Tu was angry, but not because of her trip to London. In fact, it was anger that drove her to England in the first place.

During the mid-eighties, Tu was shattered when she could not pass the matriculation examination the first time. She had to repeat the standard until she passed.

"The (apartheid) system in South Africa had made me doubt myself. By going to London, I wanted to do something that would make my presence felt (in the world)," she explains.

After her return from London, she was kept busy with frequent overseas trips on singing engagements. Then she decided to contact the famous Manhattan School of Music in the United States. She was hungry for music education and for a boost for her fledgling career.

On audition day at the school things went haywire. Tu could not understand why she had to audition just to enroll at the school.

But then something happened: the adjudicators asked her to play her guitar.

"I took my guitar and played, even though I could not read music. They asked me to play a jazz standard and wanted to know in what key I was playing. I had no idea."

During her second song, a composition she had done while in Chicago, one of the adjudicators left the room. Afterwards the same person was waiting for her outside with an offer of a scholarship. She had to pay half of her fees herself, though. But the main thing was, Tu had made an impression at a highly respected academic institution.

Unfortunately, the struggle proved too much. Money was scarce and Tu had to drop out of music school. She returned to South Africa. Not empty-handed, however. While she was in the United States she wrote a journal about the life of her musician-mother, Patty, and prepared it for a show. As soon as she got back in 1992, arrangements were made and soon the show, *Singing the Times*, opened at the Market Theatre in Johannesburg.

"I hate fear," this dynamic woman explains. "When the going gets tough, I never back off. Instead, I always think God is preparing me for greater things. Call it turning a lemon into lemonade."

Tu had a headstart in her music career. She comes from a family that has been dubbed "the Jacksons of Africa" after the talented American Jackson family who produced no fewer than seven musicians in one generation. Five members of the Nokwe family are musicians and have made music their life: Tu's parents Alfred and Patty, her sister Marilyn, her younger brother Papi and herself.

Tu loves to tell of growing up in a house that was always filled with music and musicians. The Nokwe home was a "halfway house" for musicians visiting Durban, a place to stay after gigs in the city or en route to another engagement. "There was a law in our house that children had to be in bed by 8 p.m.," Tu recalls. "We had to leave the elders to socialise and discuss serious business. At the same time, the elders used to play music. There was the music of Miriam Makeba, Letta Mbulu and many others.

"Many a time I would wake up and ask to be allowed to sing along. On the occasions when I was given permission to sing for our visitors, I was the star."

Although influenced by the work of the late Ella Fitzgerald and Sarah Vaughan, Tu's parents had the biggest musical impact in her life. Other influences include pianist-saxophonist Bheki Mseleku, now a music teacher at the University of Natal in Durban, who in the nineties won fame in jazz circles in the UK and the United States for outstanding work. Before he left for the UK in the late eighties, he used to be a regular visitor at the Nokwe home.

And how would Tu like to be remembered?

"As somebody who loved to laugh and who loved children," she replies, laughing heartily. Laughter lights up her face and reminds you of Pampata, King Shaka's lover, the part she played in the blockbuster TV series *Shaka Zulu* in 1987.

Long may she laugh.

Interviewed at her home in Johannesburg, 1997

Vicky Sampson

One night thirteen years ago stands out vividly in Vicky Sampson's mind. On that cold and lonely night in 1984 she was with her mother at Johannesburg's Club 58, in the once trendy and cosmopolitan suburb of Hillbrow. There they met singer Tandie Klaasen, who was working at the club.

"When we met Tandie we were desolate. And she offered us a place to stay at her house for a week," Vicky says. She will never forget the moment. She had gone to Johannesburg to try her luck in the clubs, but things didn't work out as planned.

"Tandie was one of the people who was there for me when I started out. I think she realises I haven't forgotten what she has done for me. I believe as women in this business we should stick together and never forget where we come from.

"I don't know what would have happened to me if I hadn't met Tandie that night."

Of course, since then her career has taken off, and there have been other women singers who have been very helpful, especially Dorothy Masuka and Sophie Mgcina.

It all started for Vicky at her birthplace, Cape Town's Hanover Park, two years earlier in 1982, when her aunt Emmy Adams entered her in the SABC's Follow That Star music contest.

She was a finalist. It was an astonishing achievement for a girl who had just finished school and who was the only black contestant. The organisers chose her to appear in the Winners' Special show on SATV 1 (at the time the "white" TV channel), which featured only the winners.

Vicky remembers: "I think it was my aunt who realised that I had talent. She took that first step for me. Of course, my mother was always there as the support,

and the knowledge of my musician-father helped as well."

At that stage of her career Vicky was emulating the singers she heard played at home – Lionel Ritchie, Randy Crawford, George Benson, Betty Wright, Joan Baez, Aretha Franklin, Roberta Flack, Anita Baker, Tracy Chapman.

"I had some strange tastes. I could sing like all of them. In those days the power of being a singer was to learn to sing a song exactly like the original artist."

At this point, Vicky remembers an incident when she was seven years old. Her father bought her a Shirley Bassey album. Two songs captured her imagination: "Never, Never" and "Day by Day". She also tried to sing like Bassey. Years later Vicky would find herself in the audience of a Bassey concert in Johannesburg.

She recalls the concert: "She, my childhood heroine, was there in the flesh. She was doing amazing things on stage. There was no meaningless jumping around the stage. No gimmicks. She had style and used her voice like an instrument. It's the voice. That's what I want from a singer."

As a finalist in Follow That Star, Vicky had to travel to the big city of Johannesburg. It was a mind-blowing experience for the young singer, flying for the first time and staying in one of the city's grandest hotels, but she adapted and picked up a lot of valuable lessons.

She quickly learnt how to communicate with people. The most valuable experience was the work she did with music teacher Norma Biagi – "It was voice lessons. It was difficult at first. She taught me things I did not know."

But who is Vicky? Who is this singer who made a clean sweep of the 1996 FNB South African Music Awards for Best Pop Album, Best Music Video and Best Female Vocalist? Who is this singer whose debut hit single, "African Dream", became the anthem of the spectacular 1996 African Cup of Nations soccer championships?

She says the real Vicky Sampson is someone who believes in the power she has been given by God.

"My voice has become an instrument for me to reach people, inspire people, give them joy. It's surprising that that was not the intention when I was growing up as a young girl. Though I was singing, I never realised that one day I would become a singer. Someone people will look up to."

This brings back memories of her Cape Town community where singing for her was always a source of happiness – at school, her youth club and community get-togethers. She was never shy about singing. It was something that came naturally.

"Everything in my life basically goes back to song."

Vicky's priority at the moment is to work hard and make things happen for her. Like the launch of her second album, *Zai*, in Europe.

Vicky is confident, because "I've learnt a lot of things in this industry – for example, discipline, timing. And, of course, respect for what I'm doing."

Interviewed at her home in Berea, Johannesburg, in 1997

Yvonne Chaka Chaka

It was in 1985 that Yvonne Chaka Chaka exploded onto the South African music scene with an overnight hit, "I'm in Love with a DJ". After only two months she came with another hit, "I Cry for Freedom", which reached double gold. Her next album, *Motherland*, went double platinum throughout Africa. Her 1990 album, *Be Proud to be African*, also had record-breaking sales.

But Yvonne's fame is not limited to South Africa. She is one of the most sought-after singers in Zimbabwe, Malawi, Zambia, Tanzania, Nigeria, Côte d'Ivoire and Uganda. In Nigeria alone, her albums have officialy sold more than 600 000 copies. Her jaunts across Africa have provoked the remark, "a Soweto star that twinkles all over the continent", and earned her the name "Princess of Africa". When this princess talks of her dreams about being a big international star, she is not to be taken lightly.

"In Africa they make me feel like a king. Not a queen, not a princess, but a king. Recently I was in Nigeria, and at the first show we had about 200 000 people. It was incredible. I was there the same week that Nelson Mandela visited the country, and I was told that I attracted more people than he did," Yvonne told the South African woman's magazine *Fair Lady* in November 1991.

Such has been her impact in Nigeria that in 1990 the giant American soft-drink company Pepsi, wanting to break into that country's soft-drink market, used her to launch their product, choosing her above Madonna.

Seeking an image that would sell Pepsi, the London-based admen chose the sexy Soweto star who was born Yvonne Ntombizodwa Machaka.

"In the end," explained the *Saturday Star*, who reported on the matter, "it boiled down to a question of who was more popular in Africa. And soon Yvonne found herself on the way to Nigeria for the filming of a television commercial that would get Pan-African exposure."

It is said the Pepsi marketing team based their choice on the following facts: Yvonne

had sold 300 000 discs within 18 months of turning professional; she had pulled 80 000 fans at a Nairobi show and entertained 200 000 people who had paid the equivalent of R45 each in the Nigerian capital, Lagos.

"Yvonne is at the pinnacle of her success in Africa and is poised for major international recognition. Her albums have already been released in Japan," the newspaper concluded.

Of course, thousands of South Africans have felt the appeal of Yvonne Chaka Chaka's public appearances. After becoming the first recipient of the coveted Harvest Music Award in 1991, for instance, she became the first artist to pack the Venda National Stadium to its 45 000 capacity.

"November 16, 1991, will go down in history as the day when 7 000 people forgot their differences and problems, converged in Sun City for two-and-a-half hours and danced to the rhythm of life," the *Star* said of one of her concerts.

In 1992 Yvonne was invited to perform at the Miss World beauty contest at Sun City in the then homeland of Bophutha-tswana. When asked to comment on the occasion during a television interview in 1993, Yvonne simply said: "It was one of the best things to happen in my life."

Nobody could doubt her as she, for a brief moment, relived the magic of the glittering contest that was beamed to more than 600 million viewers in sixty countries. She had shared the stage with, among others, top South African singers Abigail Kubeka and Mara Louw – not to mention VIPs like American socialite Ivana Trump, actor Billy Dee Williams and screen star Joan Collins.

But Yvonne has not forgotten where she comes from; nor has she forgotten the pioneering women singers. She told the *Sowetan* in 1991: "Any work of art needs to be saved for posterity. Artists who were in their prime long before some of us were born, deserve to be heard. Young ones can learn a lot from them."

Adding: "I'm also honoured to have my work in the same collection as Miriam Makeba, who is my major inspiration. She is all that one aspires to in a true African woman."

Yvonne, who heads her own promotions company, says about ballads, her favourite kind of music: "Yes, my ballads have a strong message. And I think that's the way it should be. Now it's even better, because you can express yourself the way you want to."

There is no doubt that Yvonne is referring to the relatively free political climate in the new South Africa that holds so much promise, and that should also help to liberate musicians.

This was perhaps the thinking of the Kenyan government when they invited her to their country's 25th independence anniversary in 1988. A statement from President arap Moi's office said Yvonne was selected on account of her popularity and "the need to sensitise people about the struggle by black people of South Africa against apartheid".

Her future?

"Oh yes, I can't wait to be a big international star. That's a dream. And I'm going to work for it, but right now the most important thing in my life is my family."

Yvonne, who in private life has been married to a medical doctor for eight years, is a mother of three children. That does not keep her from also dedicating time to her her music and charity work. In her showpiece five-bedroom house in the upmarket Johannesburg suburb of Bryanston, she has entertained people who have included President Nelson Mandela and American actress Joan Collins.

Compiled from broadcast and published sources in 1997

Yvonne Martins

At the height of her music career she was known by thousands of music lovers as "Tornado". Comedian Louis Peterson, who coined the name, used to say that she came on stage like a tornado when she sang.

The name fitted Yvonne Martins of the Gay Gaities like a glove. Frequently sharing the stage with hot performers like the Manhattan Brothers, the African Inkspots, the Harlem Swingsters and singers of Dolly Rathebe's calibre, assured Yvonne and the rest of her group of the status they richly deserved.

"We were a top song and dance variety group, consisting of up to fifteen performers at any given time. And we always packed them into venues like the Bantu Men's Social Centre and the East Rand's Davey Social Centre," Yvonne recalls.

The Gaities differed in many respects from the legion of musicians providing entertainment in the fifties, particularly in the vibrant Sophiatown where Yvonne Martins was born and grew up. What made the group stand out was that they sang Latin-American pieces, with tap dancing and jazz to spice up their acts.

That approach and presentation assured the Gay Gaities of a place in the entertainment world, despite tough competition. Hence it was an honour for any talented youngster to win a place in the Gaities.

Though Yvonne grew up in a musical family, her parents wanted her to follow a nursing career after school. But the stage-struck Yvonne would have nothing of that. She wanted to sing, and she finally called on the Gaities manager, James Tutie, to audition for a place in the company.

"In those days, you had to become a teacher or a nurse. But that wasn't me, that was not what I wanted to do. So my parents were not that terribly supportive of my career choice," Yvonne says.

The turning point came when the Gaities got stranded in Cape Town while they were on tour. In the group, Yvonne remembers, was fellow trouper General Duze, probably the most prominent African jazz guitarist in the fifties, which illustrates the high standard of the Cape Town show.

"When we came back to Sophiatown, I was done with school. I was sticking with show business."

So began a torrid ten-year love affair for Yvonne and the Gaities. She gave herself body and soul to her music. Today she is constantly reminded of that period of her life by her eldest daughter Gay, named in honour of the Gaities.

Performing with the Gaities and working with some of the biggest names in the trade had its ups and downs. But Yvonne took it all in her stride.

"Sometimes we had to go for months on end without pay. But for the love of music and what we were doing, we soldiered on. In its strange way it was fun."

Of course there was also an ugly side to being a musician then, especially in places like Sophiatown. But the Gaities were fortunate. Crime and thugs, the bane of a musician's life, never really bothered them. And in Sophiatown the Gaities were virtually adopted by the one gang, the Americans.

"The Gaities were loved by the Americans. They looked after us, especially during and after performances. We had to have people guarding the girls in our group as there was a tendency by the gangsters to break up shows and take away girls to the notorious Alexandra township."

The one thing that has always made Martin's choice of career worthwhile for her has been the audiences. She says that audiences were warmer then, and highly appreciative. This, she believes, touched musicians to such an extent that most of them were not in the business for money.

"There were many interesting times. To me, looking back now, it seems as if most of our shows were fantastic. Each had a character of its own. There was this show we shared with the Manhattan Brothers, Inkspots and our main rivals, the Synco Fans under Wilfred Sentsho, at the Bantu Men's Social Centre. That

show confirmed that we were reckoned as the best outfit in the business." Yvonne swears that that particular show will forever linger in her memory.

She also remembers the top musicians who made it all worthwhile. There was her favourite group, the Woody Woodpeckers, and the Harlem Swingsters.

The painful part comes when Yvonne tells how her career was ended. In the fifties the Nationalist Party government, which came into power in 1948, intensified its apartheid policy. It crippled African artistic life. The Group Areas Act, which determined that Africans lived with Africans and so-called Coloureds with Coloureds, meant that groups like the Gay Gaities, with its mixture of Africans and Coloureds, were doomed to die.

The death knell finally sounded when Sophiatown was declared a white residential area in 1955. Yvonne and her grandmother moved to Soweto, and she and a few members of the Gaities valiantly tried to revive the magic of their group with the help of composer and talent scout Vandi Leballo.

"We tried to bring back the Gaities in 1960, but it just didn't work. The Group Areas Act killed our company."

Yvonne bemoans the fact that today most musicians are in the game for money, and that many of them consequently lack quality and do not last.

For her, talk of music quality brings back memories of the dedication and care for music during her Gaities era. Those Gaities who already worked or were still at school never missed the afternoon rehearsals at their Western Township headquarters in Paul Malunga Street.

"On Saturdays and Sundays, if we had no shows, we spent the whole day rehearsing. We worked out all the difficult routines of our acts. As a result, Mr James Tutie's house in Western Native Township was like home," Yvonne says, and her voice betrays longing for a lost era.

Even though she has been out of music for almost thirty years, Yvonne is very sure of one thing: "If I had to live my life all over, I would do it again."

Interviewed at her home in Eden Park, Johannesburg, in 1993

Zakithi Dlamini

Even the passionate pleading of her parents to first finish high school could not persuade a teenage Zakithi Dlamini to abandon a promising career in music. No power on earth could stand in her way as she relentlessly pursued her dream of becoming a singer, even after her parents had taken her out of playwright Gibson Kente's 1963 musical, *Manana the Jazz Prophet*.

"When my parents took me out of the musical I went back to school. But my heart was set on a career as a singer."

Kente had not forgotten her. When their paths eventually crossed again a few years later, it was just in time for the opening of his second musical, *Sikalo*, in 1966.

"Without hesitation I joined Kente and managed to win my parents over to my way of thinking. They were agreeable, and supported me to continue my career."

Zakithi had started her career some years earlier in the company of some of the top stars in the music industry, and now, armed with loads of ambition, there was no stopping her.

She had already shown talent at an early age as a student at the St Louis Catholic Convent in Newcastle, KwaZulu-Natal. In 1956, when Africans were forcibly removed from their homes in the "mixed" suburb of Sophiatown where Zakithi's parents were living at the time, the family were moved to Meadowlands in Soweto. Hence Zakithi attended school at the nearby Orlando.

It was in Orlando that she met and befriended singer Busi (Viccie) Mhlongo, who was then a rising star for the mass-selling record label Big Beat.

"Viccie and her friends used to fetch me from my school in Orlando to help them out with their music and recordings," Zakithi recalls.

During a working stint with Viccie, the teenaged Zakithi's fortune was to change because she made an important connection in the recording industry: she was introduced to talent scout Sam Alcock from the Gallo recording company. Alcock wasted no time and teamed her

up with Snowy Peterson and Nomonde Sihawu to form a trio.

She cannot remember the name, but the group was an instant success, and there followed the inevitable tour of the country's major cities.

"During our tour we met a number of talent scouts, among others Dan Poho of Union Artists. He snapped me up for a variety show, *Township Tempo*, that they were mounting. This was a breakthrough in itself, because I worked with real pros and heavyweights like Abigail Kubeka and Sophie Mgcina." The memory still excites Zakithi.

At Dorkay House, where Union Artists, occupied office and rehearsal space, Zakithi met Kente for the second time. After this significant meeting, she devoted more than twenty years to Kente's work, charting new territories in South Africa's musical theatre and becoming the longest-serving artist in the Kente stable.

During a break from her work with Kente, Zakithi met impresario Bertha Egnos, who employed her in the show *Lulu Wena*. After the South African run, they toured Canada but renamed the show *Two Faces of Africa*.

"In Canada our show was heavily picketed. Canadians were against the show which they said gave a distorted picture of apartheid in South Africa. The show lasted three weeks and had to close down. Some of the cast members remained behind and sought political asylum in Canada." After all these years the recollection still brings a bitter expression to her face.

Immediately after touching home soil, Zakithi joined Kente again, and in 1993 she played a major role in his *Mfowethu*, a ground-breaking work produced in

Bloemfontein under the aegis of PACOFS (Performing Arts Council of the Orange Free State).

However, in between her work with Kente, she did plenty of drama work for the fledgling African language channels of SABC-TV. Zakithi has warm memories of the hit *uDeliwe*, which featured the late screen actor Simon Sabela.

"In fact, *uDeliwe* Part One, Two and Three gave me substantial exposure and work in television. There were also minor parts in a number of films," she says.

What drives Zakithi in her career?

There is no doubt in her mind: music. She inherited her love for music from her mother; American greats like Sarah Vaughan and Mahalia Jackson prove to have been major influences early in her career.

When Zakithi performs, she becomes oblivious to anything and anybody. Her music is her life, and her voice is her most valuable asset. If she has not done any voice training for a few days, she feels guilty. She echoes master pianist Arthur Rubinstein when he says: "If I omit to practice one day, I notice it. If two days, my friends notice it; if three days, the public notices it. It is the old doctrine – practice makes perfect."

How does she feel about the present state of music in South Africa?

Zakithi believes that good things are going to happen to local musicians, and that there is a trend to return to old-style music.

However, there is a tinge of sadness in Zakithi's voice when she observes that most female musicians of her generation and before have nothing to show for their efforts.

"We 'old girls' have been pushed aside. Even children we trained in the trade have moved fast and can readily show the rewards of their toil. No wonder that our community is asking why we are poor after so many years in show business."

The words don't come easily, but Zakithi refuses to be defeated.

Interviewed at her Meadowlands home, Soweto, in 1994

SOURCES

The author wishes to acknowledge his
indebtedness to the following sources:

GENERAL:
Just the Ticket! My 50 Years in Show Business Percy Tucker.
  Johannesburg: Jonathan Ball, 1997.
Marabi Nights: Early South African Jazz and Vaudeville
  Christopher Ballantine. Johannesburg: Ravan Press, 1993.
Miriam Makeba and the Skylarks African Heritage Series
  Volumes 1 & 2, Sleeve notes by Rob Allingham. Teal
  Records, 1991.
The Fifties People of South Africa Compiled and edited by Jurgen
  Schadenberg. Johannesburg: Bailey's African Photo Archives,
  1987.

ABIGAIL KUBEKA:
Pace magazine, June 1992.

BRENDA FASSIE:
City Press, 1 September 1991; 10 November 1991;
  24 April 1994.
Drum magazine, October 1995.
Sowetan, 4 July 1991; 18 November 1991; 8 November 1993.
The Star, 11 November 1993.
The Star Tonight, 27 May 1992; 13 December 1992;
  6 January 1997.
Sunday Times, 13 March 1994.
Sunday Times Extra, 13 December 1992.
Vrye Weekblad, 13 December 1992.
Weekly Mail, 6 June 1990; 15 January 1993.
Who's Really Who in South Africa. Hilary Prendini Toffoli and
  Gus Silber. Johannesburg: Jonathan Ball, 1989.

BUSI (VICCIE) MHLONGO:
The World, 12 May 1962.

DOLLY RATHEBE:
The World, 3 November 1967.

DOROTHY MASUKA:
Two Tone magazine *(Vrye Weekblad),* 30 April 1992.

ISABELLA MASOTE:
1992 Sowetan-Caltex Massed Choirs Festival, Programme
  notes.

LETTA MBULU:
Press hand-out issued by Word of Mouth Productions, 1990.
The Star Tonight, 30 July 1992.

MAHOTELLA QUEENS:
New Nation, 12 February 1992.

MARA LOUW:
Programme notes for the musical *King Afrika,* 1988.

MARGARET SINGANA (MCINGANA):
Biographical notes issued by Mike Fuller Music (Pty) Ltd, 1993.

MIRIAM MAKEBA:
"Miriam Makeba: Self Portrait" on Radio South Africa,
  12 December 1991.
African Rock: The Pop Music of a Continent Chris Stapleton and
  Chris May. New York: Obelisk/Dutton, 1990.

PATTY NOKWE:
The Star Tonight, 1 December 1992.
Sunday Star, 22 November 1992.

REBECCA MALOPE:
Biographical notes issued by T. Musicman, Johannesburg,
  July 1997.
City Press, 17 December 1989; 20 October 1991.
Learn and Teach magazine, 5 February 1992.
Sowetan, 12 November 1990; 9 July 1991; 16 April 1992.
Sunday Times, 14 October 1990; March 24, 1991.
Sunday Times Magazine, 24 March 1991.

SIBONGILE KHUMALO:
1992 Sowetan-Caltex Massed Choirs Festival, Programme
  notes.
Sunday Times TV Times, 29 November 1992.

SOPHIE MGCINA:
"Torn from Body and Soul" in *Time* magazine, 4 January 1993.

STELLA STARR:
The Star Tonight, 18 March 1993.

SUSAN GABASHANE:
Zonk! magazine, June 1959.

THEMBI MTSHALI:
SABC-TV publicity hand-out, August 1985.
The Star Tonight, 21 July 1997.

YVONNE CHAKA CHAKA:
SABC-TV CCV "Z-D" programme, 1 February 1993.
City Press, 30 June 1988; 11 November 1990.
Saturday Star, 28 July 1990.
The Star, 13 July 1990.
The Star Tonight, 9 October 1991.
Sowetan, 14 October 1988; 11 May 1992.

ZAKITHI DLAMINI:
In Township Tonight: South Africa's Black City Music and Theatre
  David B Coplan. Johannesburg: Ravan Press, 1985.

Glossary of African Music Terms

African jazz – A South African variant of American big band swing which developed in township halls during the forties. Although the American swing rhythm is retained, the melodies and short, repetitive harmonic cycles are South African. During the fifties this type of music was also called mbaqanga and majuba, and today is sometimes referred to as township jazz. The best known contemporary exponents of African Jazz are the Elite Swingsters and the African Jazz Pioneers.

afro-fusion – A "cross-over" style which fuses "traditional" African musical elements with jazz.

amahubo – Traditional Zulu regimental anthems accompanied by slow forceful, synchronised dancing.

gumboot dance – A dance style performed in rubber Wellington boots in which dancers produce complicated rhythms by clapping, stamping and slapping their boots. It is associated with mine, dock and municipal workers in Durban and Johannesburg.

isicathamiya or *mbube* or *ngom' ebusuku* – A male-voice a cappella choral style developed during the thirties by Zulu migrants living in hostels in Natal and Johannesburg. The term isicathamiya derives from the Zulu word meaning to stalk or step softly, which describes the dance routines performed by the choristers. This style is also called *mbube* because the first song in this genre to achieve widespread acclaim was "Mbube", recorded by Solomon Linda's Original Evening Birds in 1939. Another term for isicathamiya is *ngom' ebusuku* because the competitions between isicathamiya choirs take place at night, as the choir members work during the day ("ubusuku" is Zulu for "night"). The best known exponents of isicathamiya are Ladysmith Black Mambazo.

isidorodo or *setolotolo* – An isiNdebele single-stringed mouth bow. The player cups his/her mouth lightly over the string, changing the shape of the mouth cavity in order to resonate different notes from the string, which is lightly tapped.

kwela – A style of pennywhistle music which developed in Johannesburg's townships during the fifties. Usually played by young boys or youths, kwela is characterised by a lilting shuffle rhythm and infectious short melodies which are repeated and varied. The most famous kwela musicians are the late Spokes Mashiyane and Lemmy "Special" Mabaso.

maskanda – A Zulu neo-traditional style played by Zulu migrant workers usually on guitar, although other instruments such as violins and concertinas are also used. A troubadour playing in this style is known as a maskandi.

mbaqanga – An instrumental style which developed from kwela and sax jive in the recording studios during the early sixties. In mbaqanga the rhythm, lead and bass guitars are electric and a strong bass line dominates. The originators and best exponents of instrumental mbaqanga are the Makhona Tsohle Band. This group accompanies the most famous exponents of vocal mbaqanga (see *mqashiyo*), Mahlatini and the Mahotella Queens. (Also see *African jazz*.)

mbube – see *isicathamiya*

mohobelo – A Basotho dance of war or merry making characterised by rhythmic singing of praise songs. Only Basotho men may participate.

mqashiyo – Vocal mbaqanga sung by a female close harmony group of three to five singers often accompanying a male vocalist called a "groaner", who bellows in an ultra deep bass voice. Another term used to describe this music is *simanje-manje* meaning now-now. Mahlatini and the Mahotella Queens are the best known exponents of this style.

ngom' ebusuku – see *isicathamiya*

setolotolo – see *isidorodo*

simanje-manje – see *mqashiyo*

township jazz – see *African jazz*

Z B MOLEFE is a journalist of wide and varied experience who, like his generation, has had special rapport with singers and other people involved in show business, particulary in the fifties and sixties. He is also the contributing editor of the current three-volume "Know Africa" encyclopaedia. In his long journalistic career he has travelled to various parts of Africa, Europe and the Unitied States, where he delived papers and studied journalism. He is also a published poet. In 1994 and 1996 he received the merit award in the Book Journalist of the Year competition. His passion is literature, theatre, music in general and jazz in particular. He is based in Johannesburg where is currently marketing manager of the Sunday newspaper *City Press*.

MIKE MZILENI started his career in photography in 1963. The next year he joined the *The World*. Subsequent to leaving this now defunct "black" newspaper in 1967, he worked for various Johannesburg-based publications: the *Golden City Post*, *Drum* magazine, the *Rand Daily Mail* (also defunct), the *Sunday Express* and the *Sunday Times* – until 1982 when he was appointed chief photographer of the *Golden City Press*, now known as *City Press*, a post he still holds. In 1966 already he was featured in a World Press Photo Competition in The Hague, Netherlands, and in 1985 he was named JPS Sports Photographer of the Year. His contribution to photography was acknowledged when he was appointed a judge in the 1996 Fuji Photo Press Awards.

LARA ALLEN began her academic career researching kwela music, for which, in 1993, she received a master's degree cum laude from the University of Natal. She has presented conference papers and conducted seminars on South African music in southern Africa, Europe and north America. Committed to making the findings of her research available beyond the confines of academia, she has written radio programmes, presented public lectures and organised concerts. She also writes about South African music for *The Star* (Johannesburg) and *Folk Roots Magazine* (UK). The recipient of several prestigious scholarship, Lara is presently engaged in doctoral research on women in black South African popular music, at the University of Cambridge.